MW00987765

THE STORY OF THE FAMILY

THE STORY OF THE FAMILY

G. K. Chesterton
on the Only State That Creates
and Loves Its Own Citizens

Edited with an Introduction
by Dale Ahlquist

IGNATIUS PRESS   SAN FRANCISCO

Cover art and design by John Herried

© 2022 by Ignatius Press, San Francisco
All rights reserved
ISBN 978-1-62164-447-7 (PB)
ISBN 978-1-64229-186-5 (eBook)
Library of Congress Catalogue Number 2021933136
Printed in the United States of America ∞

CONTENTS

PRELUDE

Defending the Triangle

By Dale Ahlquist

You can free things from alien or accidental laws, but not from the laws of their own nature. You may, if you like, free a tiger from his bars; but do not free him from his stripes. Do not free a camel of the burden of his hump: you may be freeing him from being a camel. Do not go about as a demagogue, encouraging triangles to break out of the prison of their three sides. If a triangle breaks out of its three sides, its life comes to a lamentable end.

—G. K. Chesterton, *Orthodoxy*

The above is a quintessential quote from Chesterton: pleasing to the ear, colorful to the eye, laced with soft humor and sharp wit, and making a point that is inescapable. We cannot free a thing from its own nature. We can only love a thing, and defend it, for being itself and not something else. When any triangle loses one of its three sides, it stops being a triangle. There is no argument about this. The same logic applies if the triangle happens to be a

This originally appeared in *Inside the Vatican*, November 2015.

family—father, mother, child. Ah, but then the arguments suddenly and ferociously begin!

It is difficult to defend the obvious. We don't even know where to begin. It is also easy to forget the obvious. Breathing only becomes an issue when we are out of breath. The family is a perfect example of something so obvious that it is difficult to defend—so obvious that it is easy to ignore. But decay begins to set in, says Chesterton, when we forget the obvious things.

When people start arguing about the triangle of the family, they dance around the definition of the thing. Yet they want to talk about nothing but exceptions, which means they are assuming the definition they do not want to discuss. In other words, the arguments about the family seem largely to ignore the family, to ignore the normal and focus on the abnormal, with earnest people making impassioned pleas about *broken* families; about unwanted children; about parents who are not married to each other; about nonparents who *are* married to each other; about the divorced and remarried; about those suffering from a same-sex attraction who simply want to be "happy" (which they claim will come from playing house); about single parents and abusive parents and absent parents. As Chesterton says, "Hardly anybody [outside a particular religious press] dares to defend the family. The world around us has accepted a social system which denies the family. It will sometimes help the child in spite of the family; the mother in spite of the family; the grandfather in spite of the family. It will not help the family."[1]

We are arguing about the frayed edges of an essential garment, and we have forgotten the purpose of that

---

[1] G. K. Chesterton (hereafter, unless otherwise noted, the author is Chesterton), *G. K.'s Weekly*, September 20, 1930.

garment. We have forgotten the basic function of the family, which makes it difficult, if not impossible, to study the anthropology of the family.

In a 1920 book called *The Superstition of Divorce*, Chesterton gets down to basics and tells us "The Story of the Family". His first three points: The family is the most ancient of human institutions. It has an authority. It is universal.

It is an institution that precedes the State. It differs from the State, and from any other institution, in that "it begins with a spontaneous attraction".[2] It is not coercive. "There is nothing in any other social relations in any way parallel to the mutual attraction of the sexes. By missing this simple point, the modern world has fallen into a hundred follies."[3]

The State regulation of marriage is one of those follies. But the political follies are only a result of cultural follies, such as feminism, which Chesterton defines as women trying to be men.[4] Such follies have led to our recent fixations on "gender confusion" and the rush to condone rather than condemn strange sexual attractions. The revolt of women against men has fueled the revolt of men against women.

Chesterton says, "These are very simple truths; that is why nobody nowadays seems to take any particular notice of them; and the truth that follows next is equally obvious. There is no dispute about the purpose of Nature in creating such an attraction. It would be more intelligent to call it the purpose of God; for Nature can have no purpose

[2] "The Story of the Family", in *The Superstition of Divorce*, in *The Collected Works of G. K. Chesterton*, vol. 4 (San Francisco: Ignatius Press, 1987), p. 252 (hereafter *CW*, followed by volume number and page number).

[3] Ibid.

[4] "Folly and Female Education", in *What's Wrong with the World*, in *CW* 4:197.

unless God is behind it. To talk of the purpose of Nature is to make a vain attempt to avoid being anthropomorphic, merely by being feminist. It is believing in a goddess because you are too sceptical to believe in a god."[5]

At the most basic natural level, "the child is an explanation of the father and mother".[6] At the more human level, the child is the explanation "of the ancient human ties connecting the father and mother".[7] Thus, the family is "the primary position of the human group".[8] It survives regimes. It survives empires. It survives civilizations. "This triangle of truisms, of father, mother and child, cannot be destroyed; it can only destroy those civilisations which disregard it."[9]

But whenever the family falters, there is only one entity with enough heft to fill its functions: the State. The State can step in as provider, educator, entertainer, counselor, caretaker. However, whenever it has to take the role as a substitute for the family, it is only a stop-gap measure at best. It cannot ultimately replace a natural process; it can only interfere with it. Any sustained attempts will be futile. We work hard enough to raise our own children. We cannot possibly raise everyone else's children. "If people cannot mind their own business, it cannot possibly be more economical to pay them to mind each other's business; and still less to mind each other's babies. It is simply throwing away a natural force and then paying for an artificial force; as if a man were to water a plant with a hose while holding up an umbrella to protect it from the rain."[10]

[5] "Story of the Family", p. 253.
[6] Ibid.
[7] Ibid.
[8] Ibid.
[9] Ibid., p. 254.
[10] Ibid.

Chesterton says that the reformers do not understand the basis of the thing they are trying to rebuild. You cannot break apart the basic unit of civilization, which is the family. You cannot replace the authority of parents. You cannot replace the bond between a husband and wife. You cannot replace the bond between a mother and child. You can only waste your time trying. And disintegration of society with the atomization of special interests, the elevation of State education, and the legalization of divorce and contraception and abortion and same-sex marriage are all of them wastes of time. The family will survive them all. The family, which came into existence without the government and has continued to exist without the support of the government, will withstand any unnatural laws made by the government. But in the meantime everyone suffers. Everyone. Because everyone is either a father or a mother or a child.

A century ago Chesterton said that the authority of the family is being undermined by an "officialism" that is based on popular science, which has a vague authority that no one can pin down and does not answer to anybody. He warns that this officialism will only become more rigid. Shortly before he died in 1936, he observed prophetically: "The frightful punishment of mere sex emancipation is not anarchy but bureaucracy."[11] His prophecy has, of course, been fulfilled with painful accuracy. The generation that would break free from the family has found itself in chains.

In the meantime, the family has gone from being ignored and neglected to being attacked and torn to pieces. What has been reassembled does not look anything like the family. The practical three-sided arrangement has been discarded for experimental models that may be official, but are not practical. "The disintegration of rational society

[11] *Illustrated London News*, January 4, 1936.

started in the drift from the hearth and the family," says Chesterton. "The solution must be a drift back."[12]

The family has always had to fight to protect itself, whether against the beast in the forest, the barbarian invader in the village, the industrial machine in the city, or the mad official in the State. It seems that everything has always been against this ancient institution of the family. Everything. With one exception. At a certain turning point in history, there arose another institution that came to the defense of the family. It not only recognized its importance; it blessed it and made it sacred. It was the Catholic Church. Nothing can destroy the sacred triangle of the family, but the Church, says Chesterton, succeeded in turning the triangle upside down: "It held up a mystical mirror in which the order of the three things was reversed; and added a holy family of child, mother and father to the human family of father, mother and child."[13]

[12] *G. K.'s Weekly*, March 30, 1933.
[13] "Story of the Family", p. 261.

INTRODUCTION

By Dale Ahlquist

There is a scene in *The Man Who Was Thursday* when the wandering poet Gabriel Syme strikes up a conversation with a policeman on a foggy evening along London's Embankment. The policeman informs Syme that a strange "purely intellectual conspiracy will soon threaten the very existence of civilization, that the scientific and artistic worlds are silently bound in a crusade against the Family."[1] He goes on to say that the "most dangerous criminal now is the entirely lawless modern philosopher".[2] These destroyers of the normal "hate life itself, their own as much as other people's".[3]

The cosmic detective story was published in 1908. Since then things have only gotten worse, but G. K. Chesterton has only gotten better. His descriptions of the dilemma are as timely and lucid as ever, but more importantly his solutions are still refreshingly spirited and pointed and completely right. Chesterton is a champion of the family in the same vein as Saint Thomas More, with the same wit and also, I am too confident to say, the same holiness. In fact, I would argue that Saint Thomas More, the glorious martyr, had a more straightforward task: he had to deal with

---

[1] *The Man Who Was Thursday*, in *CW*, vol. 6 (San Francisco: Ignatius Press, 1991), p. 508.
[2] Ibid., p. 509.
[3] Ibid.

only one mad, murderous king, whereas Chesterton takes on a whole mad, murderous culture unknowingly infected with a philosophy that hates life itself. "We are no longer in a world in which it is thought normal to be moderate or even necessary to be normal. Most men now are not so much rushing to extremes as merely sliding to extremes; and even reaching the most violent extremes by being almost entirely passive.... We can no longer trust even the normal man to value and guard his own normality."[4] Chesterton's great task is to defend the normal. His great gift is to explain the obvious to a world that has utterly lost track of it. He strikes like lightning on a landscape that has gone dark.

Family, love, marriage, babies, parents, and the home are normal things. The world respects none of these things. It is off-kilter and abnormal, and yet it presumes to teach the family. Sex has been separated from love, from marriage, from birth, and has not only lost its chief purpose, but has been asserted against it. The classroom and the office— two places where most normal people hate to be—have become more important than the home, which is where any normal person would prefer to be.

One of the most difficult things to defend or even describe or discuss is the obvious thing. So Chesterton has to get us to see this familiar thing as a strange thing so that we can see it, really see it, possibly for the first time. So he starts by asking us to imagine going to a random city, to a random street, to a random house, and going down the chimney and then trying to get along with the people who are living there. That, he says, is what happens to each of us on the day we are born. That is how we enter a family. In a family, we have to get along with a group of people we did

[4] *America*, January 4, 1936.

not choose to live with, which happens to be the same situation in our relationship with the rest of the world: "The men and women who, for good reasons and bad, revolt against the family, are, for good reasons and bad, simply revolting against mankind."[5]

The ridiculously obvious point is that marriage is the natural basis for raising children; if we destroy marriage through divorce, we take away from children the stability they deserve. We destroy the family. The war on the family begins with the attack on marriage, then on the marriage act, then on children—first through killing children in the womb or on the delivery table, then by killing the innocence without killing the child—and then on the soul through an education system that has banished God. We must also mention the attack on the home through a political and economic system that has attempted to dissolve the two most basic human relations that have traditionally provided the most natural satisfaction: the relationship between a husband and wife, and the relationship between a mother and child. These two relations, says Chesterton, "are also the only two recognized combinations in capitalist civilization which that system has set out to destroy".[6]

"Capitalist civilization"? Didn't expect that. But Chesterton's argument is that the wage system that has pulled both father and mother out of the home, working for someone else rather than for themselves, has broken up the family. And when the family fails, only one force is strong enough to replace it: the State. This is why capitalism and socialism are in cahoots: big government, which

[5] "On Certain Modern Writers and the Institution of the Family", in *Heretics*, in *CW*, vol. 1 (San Francisco: Ignatius Press, 1986), pp. 141–42.

[6] *New Witness*, October 21, 1921.

Chesterton calls Hudge, and big business, which Chesterton calls Gudge, have conspired against Jones, the common man.

It is important to note that Chesterton's argument represents a comprehensive and cohesive philosophy: there is a connection between big business and birth control, between the rise of public education and the decline of parenthood.

In 1968, Saint Pope Paul VI issued perhaps the most important encyclical of the twentieth century: *Humanae Vitae.* He warned that contraception would lead to divorce, to abortion, to infanticide, to sexual perversion. He was right. But G. K. Chesterton made all the same warnings a generation earlier. He was right. However, he saw contraception as only part of the plot against the family. There was a larger force at work, and Chesterton understood this by drawing on the encyclical of an earlier pope: Leo XIII's 1891 *Rerum Novarum*, which formed the basis of Catholic social teaching and has been affirmed by every pope since. It was Pope Leo who first argued that our entire modern social and economic structure undermines the family, that industrial capitalism had produced conditions almost worse than slavery, and that the reaction against it, socialism, was just as bad. The just solution was for more workers to become owners. He was right. Chesterton expanded on Pope Leo's ideas. He argued that the capitalist Gudge, with his emphasis on individual interests, and the socialist Hudge, with his emphasis on the State or community interests, are enemies of Mr. and Mrs. Jones and all the Jones' babies. A sane society is based on the family's interests because the family is the basic unit of society.

It was the Church's social teaching that was the closing argument in convincing G. K. Chesterton to become a Catholic. In 1922, on the eve of his conversion, he wrote a letter to his mother, saying: "I am convinced ... that the fight for the family and the free citizen and everything decent must now be waged by the one fighting form of Christianity."[7] He wanted to join the Church that would fight for the family. For the rest of his life, he fought for the faith and for the family.

Chesterton's philosophy of distributism continues to be dismissed, and it does not go away. The main point of distributism is that everything starts local. A family-run business is part of a family-run world. It is a bottom-up solution. The city's functions are secondary to the home's functions. The school is a preparation for the home, not the home a mere dropping-off place for the school. If we take care of our families, we take care of the world. And if we have families, we have the world.

The opening sentence of *The Everlasting Man* is "There are two ways of getting home and one of them is to stay there."[8] Chesterton could almost have stopped writing the book right there. But he had to discuss the other way of getting home, and it involved the whole history of the world, which includes art, food, horses, swords, tribes, towers, temples, and a cross on a hill. But all the characters in that story are trying to get home.

There are those in the world who defend the home because they've never left. But then there are the rest of us who have had to discover the home through having left it and going around the world and arriving there again. The ultimate destination of every journey is home.

---

[7] From a letter quoted in Maisie Ward, *Gilbert Keith Chesterton* (New York: Sheed and Ward, 1943), p. 466.

[8] *The Everlasting Man*, in *CW*, vol. 7 (San Francisco: Ignatius Press, 2005), p. 226.

The Family ... and the World

The House of Christmas

There fared a mother driven forth
Out of an inn to roam;
In the place where she was homeless
All men are at home.
The crazy stable close at hand,
With shaking timber and shifting sand,
Grew a stronger thing to abide and stand
Than the square stones of Rome.

For men are homesick in their homes,
And strangers under the sun,
And they lay their heads in a foreign land
Whenever the day is done.
Here we have battle and blazing eyes,
And chance and honour and high surprise,
But our homes are under miraculous skies
Where the yule tale was begun.

A Child in a foul stable,
Where the beasts feed and foam;
Only where He was homeless
Are you and I at home;
We have hands that fashion and heads that
    know,
But our hearts we lost—how long ago!

In a place no chart nor ship can show
Under the sky's dome.

This world is wild as an old wives' tale,
And strange the plain things are,
The earth is enough and the air is enough
For our wonder and our war;
But our rest is as far as the fire-drake swings
And our peace is put in impossible things
Where clashed and thundered unthinkable wings
Round an incredible star.

To an open house in the evening
Home shall men come,
To an older place than Eden
And a taller town than Rome.
To the end of the way of the wandering star,
To the things that cannot be and that are,
To the place where God was homeless
And all men are at home.

Christianity was always a domestic religion. It began with
the Holy Family.

— *Illustrated London News*, July 5, 1919

Hardly anybody (outside a particular religious press) dares
to defend the family. The world around us has accepted
a social system which denies the family. It will sometimes
help the child in spite of the family; the mother in spite
of the family; the grandfather in spite of the family. It will
not help the family.

— *G.K.'s Weekly*, September 20, 1930

To make the human family happy is the only possible
object of all education, as of all civilization.

— *The Merry-Go-Round*, June 1924

We can say that the family is the unit of the state; it is the cell that makes up the formation.

— "Professors and Prehistoric Men", *The Everlasting Man*

The Family is much more of a fact even than the State.

— *Illustrated London News*, February 20, 1909

The mere word "Science" is already used as a sacred and mystical word in many matters of politics and ethics. It is already used vaguely to threaten the most vital traditions of civilisation—the family and the freedom of the citizen.

— *Illustrated London News*, October 9, 1920

The first things must be the very fountains of life, love and birth and babyhood; and these are always covered fountains, flowing in the quiet courts of the home.

— "The Eclipse of Liberty", *Eugenics and Other Evils*

Only men to whom the family is sacred will ever have a standard by which to criticize the state.

— "The War of Gods and Demons",
The Everlasting Man

The family as a corporate conception has already faded into the background, and is in danger of fading from the background.

— "The Family and the Feud", *Irish Impressions*

The modern world changes its philosophy as often as the modern heroine changes her husband. We have consistently maintained that the family is essential to all social construction in the world of fact. But it is hardly less true that it is essential even to artistic construction in the world of fiction. The family is not only a foundation for a house; it is also a frame for a portrait.

— *G. K.'s Weekly*, September 10, 1927

There is an attack on the family; and the only thing to do with an attack is to attack it.

— *G. K.'s Weekly*, October 5, 1929

As it is human to cover the body for decoration and dignity, so it is human to cover the family life with wall and roof, for privacy and domesticity.

— *G. K.'s Weekly*, July 19, 1930

The family is not a catchword; it is a concrete and objective institution with definite limits and liberties; producing, wherever it is dominant, definite tests of authority or inheritance and a particular type of popular morality.

— *New Witness*, April 6, 1923

The scientific and artistic worlds are silently bound in a crusade against the Family and the State.

— "The Tale of a Detective",
The Man Who Was Thursday

Most human experience goes to show that the more a family is really a family the better it is—that is, the more it really consists of father, mother, and children.

— *Illustrated London News*, April 3, 1909

We are no longer in a world in which it is thought normal to be moderate or even necessary to be normal. Most men now are not so much rushing to extremes as merely sliding to extremes; and even reaching the most violent extremes by being almost entirely passive.... We can no longer trust even the normal man to value and guard his own normality.

— *America*, January 4, 1936

The family is the test of freedom; because the family is the only thing that the free man makes for himself and by himself. Other institutions must largely be made for him by strangers, whether the institutions be despotic or democratic. There is no other way of organizing mankind which can give this power and dignity, not only to mankind but to men.

— "A Defence of Dramatic Unities",
Fancies vs. Fads

A man is far more closely linked with the life of nature by loving his own children than by attempting to yearn over the youthful boa constrictor or dandle the infant rhinoceros.

— *Daily News*, August 7, 1901

To control family life, for instance, you must have at least one police spy for every family. Police spies are now a minority (though I fear an increasing minority) because it has hitherto been calculated—and not, perhaps, with too rosy an optimism—that criminals will be a minority. Once make a thing which any man may do a crime, and every man must have a "shadowing" detective as every man has a shadow. Yet this is precisely the preposterous end to which are directed most modern projects of "social reform" which select things like drink, diet, hygiene, and sexual selection. If men cannot govern themselves in these things separately, it is physically impossible for them to govern themselves in these things collectively. It not only means publicity instead of privacy; it means every man in his public capacity being in charge of every other man in his private capacity. It not only means washing dirty linen in public; it means all of us living by taking in each other's washing.

— *Illustrated London News*, June 9, 1917

There will be more, not less, respect for human rights if they can be treated as divine rights.

— *Illustrated London News*, January 13, 1912

False science and quack psychology is being used to destroy that natural authority and Christian tradition of the home.

— *New Witness*, August 26, 1921

If you want the common man to fight, you must be offering him the thing for which he fights best—his own honour and his own home.

— *New Age*, April 15, 1909

The sword considered as a symbol would be a symbol of precisely those rights of the citizen which are now most necessary and most neglected. It would stand for the idea that he has in the last resort the right to defend his family individually, as to defend his country collectively.

— *Illustrated London News*, January 1, 1921

The Holy Family is in danger of insult; not even because it is holy, but merely because it is a family.

— *New Witness*, December 10, 1920

Where History Begins[*]

We shall never return to social sanity till we begin at the beginning. We must start where all history starts, with a man and a woman, and a child, and with the province of liberty and property which these need for their full humanity. As it is, we begin where history ends, or, rather, where disjointed journalism ends. We stop suddenly with the accidental truncation of today's news; and judge everything by the particular muddle of the moment.

The Story of the Family[†]

The most ancient of human institutions has an authority that may seem as wild as anarchy. Alone among all such institutions it begins with a spontaneous attraction; and may be said strictly and not sentimentally to be founded on love instead of fear. The attempt to compare it with coercive institutions complicating later history has led to infinite illogicality in later times. It is as unique as it is universal. There is nothing in any other social relations in any way parallel to the mutual attraction of the sexes. By missing this simple point, the modern world has fallen into a hundred follies. The idea of a general revolt of women against men has been proclaimed with flags and processions, like a revolt of vassals against their lords, of slaves against slave-drivers, of Poles against Prussians or Irishmen against Englishmen; for all the world as if we really believed in the fabulous nation of the Amazons. The equally philosophical idea of a general revolt of men against women has

---

*Excerpt was originally published in *Illustrated London News*, May 3, 1919.
† "The Story of the Family", in *The Superstition of Divorce*, in *CW* 4:252–61.

been put into a sociological book. But at the first touch of this truth of an aboriginal attraction, all such comparisons collapse and are seen to be comic. A Prussian does not feel from the first that he can only be happy if he spends his days and nights with a Pole. An Englishman does not think his house empty and cheerless unless it happens to contain an Irishman. A white man does not in his romantic youth dream of the perfect beauty of a black man. A railway magnate seldom writes poems about the personal fascination of a railway porter. All the other revolts against all the other relations are reasonable and even inevitable, because those relations are originally only founded upon force or self-interest. Force can abolish what force can establish; self-interest can terminate a contract when self-interest has dictated the contract. But the love of man and woman is not an institution that can be abolished, or a contract that can be terminated. It is something older than all institutions or contracts, and something that is certain to outlast them all. All the other revolts are real, because there remains a possibility that the things may be destroyed, or at least divided. You can abolish capitalists; but you cannot abolish males. Prussians can go out of Poland or negroes can be repatriated to Africa; but a man and a woman must remain together in one way or another; and must learn to put up with each other somehow.

These are very simple truths; that is why nobody now-adays seems to take any particular notice of them; and the truth that follows next is equally obvious. There is no dispute about the purpose of Nature in creating such an attraction. It would be more intelligent to call it the purpose of God; for Nature can have no purpose unless God is behind it. To talk of the purpose of Nature is to make a vain attempt to avoid being anthropomorphic, merely by being feminist. It is believing in a goddess because you are too sceptical to believe in a god. But this is a controversy which can be kept apart from the question, if we content ourselves with saying that the vital value ultimately found in this attraction is, of course, the renewal of the race itself. The child is an explanation of the father and mother; and the fact that it is a human child is the explanation of the ancient human ties connecting the father and mother. The more human, that is the less bestial, is the child, the more lawful and lasting are the ties. So far from any progress in culture or the sciences tending to loosen the bond, any such progress must logically tend to tighten it. The more things there are for the child to learn, the longer he must remain at the natural school for learning them; and the longer his teachers must at least postpone the dissolution of their partnership. This elementary truth is hidden to-day in vast masses of vicarious, indirect and artificial work, with the fundamental fallacy of which I shall deal in a moment. Here I speak of the primary position of the human group, as it has stood through unthinkable ages of waxing and waning civilisations; often unable to delegate any of its work, always unable to delegate all of it. In this, I repeat, it will always be necessary for the two teachers to remain together, in proportion as they have anything to teach. One of the shapeless sea-beasts, that merely detaches itself from its offspring and floats away, could float away to a submarine divorce court, or an advanced club founded on free-love for fishes. The sea-beast might do this, precisely because the sea-beast's offspring need do nothing; because it has not got to learn the polka or the multiplication table. All these are truisms but they are also truths, and truths that will return; for the present tangle of semi-official substitutes is not only a stop-gap, but one that is not big enough to stop the gap. If people cannot mind their own business, it cannot possibly be more economical to pay them to mind each other's business; and still less to mind each other's babies. It is simply throwing away a natural force and then paying for an artificial force; as if a man were to water a plant with a hose while holding up an umbrella to protect it from the rain. The whole really rests on a plutocratic illusion of an infinite supply of servants. When we offer any other system as a "career for women," we are really proposing that an infinite number of them should become servants, of a plutocratic or bureaucratic sort. Ultimately, we are arguing that a woman should not be a mother to her own baby, but a nursemaid to somebody else's baby. But it will not work, even on paper. We cannot all live by taking in each other's washing, especially in the form of pinafores. In the last resort, the only people who either can or will give individual care, to each of the individual children, are their individual parents. The expression as applied to those dealing with changing crowds of children is a graceful and legitimate flourish of speech.

This triangle of truisms, of father, mother and child, cannot be destroyed; it can only destroy those civilisations which disregard it. Most modern reformers are merely bottomless sceptics, and have no basis on which to rebuild; and it is well that such reformers should realise that there is something they cannot reform. You can put down the mighty from their seat; you can turn the world upside down, and there is much to be said for the view that it may then be the right way up. But you cannot create a world in which the baby carries the mother. You cannot create a world in which the mother has not authority over the baby. You can waste your time in trying; by giving votes to babies or proclaiming a republic of infants in arms. You can say, as an educationist said the other day, that small children should "criticise, question authority and suspend their judgment." I do not know why he did not go on to say that they should earn their own living, pay income tax to the state, and die in battle for the fatherland; for the proposal evidently is that children shall have no childhood. But you can, if you find entertainment in such games, organise "representative government" among little boys and girls, and tell them to take their legal and constitutional responsibilities as seriously as possible. In short, you can be crazy; but you cannot be consistent. You cannot really carry your own principle back to the aboriginal group, and really apply it to the mother and the baby. You will not act on your own theory in the simplest and most practical of all possible cases. You are not quite so mad as that.

This nucleus of natural authority has always existed in the midst of more artificial authorities. It has always been regarded as something in the literal sense individual; that is, as an absolute that could not really be divided. A baby was not even a baby apart from its mother; it was something else, most probably a corpse. It was always recognised as standing in a peculiar relation to government; simply because it was one of the few things that had not been made by government; and could to some extent come into existence without the support of government. Indeed the case for it is too strong to be stated. For the case for it is that there is nothing like it; and we can only find faint parallels to it in those more elaborate and painful powers and institutions that are its inferiors. Thus the only way of conveying it is to compare it to a nation; although, compared to it, national divisions are as modern and formal as national anthems. Thus I may often use the metaphor of a city; though in its presence a citizen is as recent as a city clerk. It is enough to note here that everybody does know by intuition and admit by implication that a family is a solid fact, having a character and colour like a nation. The truth can be tested by the most modern and most daily experiences. A man does say "That is the sort of thing the Browns will like"; however tangled and interminable a psychological novel he might compose on the shades of difference between Mr. and Mrs. Brown. A woman does say "I don't like Jemima seeing so much of the Robinsons"; and she does not always, in the scurry of her social or domestic duties, pause to distinguish the optimistic materialism of Mrs. Robinson from the more acid cynicism which tinges the hedonism of Mr. Robinson. There is a colour of the household inside, as conspicuous as the colour of the house outside. That colour is a blend, and if any tint in it predominate it is generally that preferred by Mrs. Robinson. But, like all composite colours, it is a separate colour; as separate as green is from blue and yellow. Every marriage is a sort of wild balance; and in every case the compromise is as unique as an eccentricity. Philanthropists walking in the slums often see the compromise in the street, and mistake it for a fight. When they interfere, they are thoroughly thumped by both parties; and serve them right, for not respecting the very institution that brought them into the world.

The first thing to see is that this enormous normality is like a mountain; and one that is capable of being a volcano. Every abnormality that is now opposed to it is like a mole-hill; and the earnest sociological organisers of it are exceedingly like moles. But the mountain is a volcano in another sense also; as suggested in that tradition of the southern fields fertilised by lava. It has a creative as well as a destructive side; and it only remains, in this part of the analysis, to note the political effect of this extra-political institution, and the political ideals of which it has been the champion; and perhaps the only permanent champion.

The ideal for which it stands in the state is liberty. It stands for liberty for the very simple reason with which this rough analysis started. It is the only one of these institutions that is at once necessary and voluntary. It is the only check on the state that is bound to renew itself as eternally as the state, and more naturally than the state. Every sane man recognises that unlimited liberty is anarchy, or rather is nonentity. The civic idea of liberty is to give the citizen a province of liberty; a limitation within which a citizen is a king. This is the only way in which truth can ever find refuge from public persecution, and the good man survive the bad government. But the good man by himself is no match for the city. There must be balanced against it another ideal institution, and in that sense an immortal institution. So long as the state is the only ideal institution the state will call on the citizen to sacrifice himself, and therefore will not have the smallest scruple in sacrificing the citizen. The state consists of coercion; and must always be justified from its own point of view in extending the bounds of coercion; as, for instance, in the case of conscription. The only thing that can be set up to check or challenge this authority is a voluntary law and a voluntary loyalty. That loyalty is the protection of liberty, in the only sphere where liberty can fully dwell. It is a principle of the constitution that the King never dies. It is the whole principle of the family that the citizen never dies. There must be a heraldry and heredity of freedom; a tradition of resistance to tyranny. A man must be not only free, but free-born.

Indeed, there is something in the family that might loosely be called anarchist; and more correctly called amateur. As there seems something almost vague about its voluntary origin, so there seems something vague about its voluntary Organisation. The most vital function it performs, perhaps the most vital function that anything can perform, is that of education; but its type of early education is far too essential to be mistaken for instruction. In a thousand things it works rather by rule of thumb than rule of theory. To take a commonplace and even comic example, I doubt if any text-book or code of rules has ever contained any directions about standing a child in a corner. Doubtless when the modern process is complete, and the coercive principle of the state has entirely extinguished the voluntary element of the family, there will be some exact regulation or restriction about the matter. Possibly it will say that the corner must be an angle of at least ninety-five degrees. Possibly it will say that the converging line of any ordinary corner tends to make a child squint. In fact I am certain that if I said casually, at a sufficient number of tea-tables, that corners made children squint, it would rapidly become a universally received dogma of popular science. For the modern world will accept no dogmas upon any authority; but it will accept any dogmas on no authority. Say that a thing is so, according to the Pope or the Bible, and it will be dismissed as a superstition without examination. But preface your remark merely with "they say" or "don't you know that?" or try (and fail) to remember the name of some professor mentioned in some newspaper; and the keen rationalism of the modern mind will accept every word you say. This parenthesis is not so irrelevent as it may appear, for it will be well to remember that when a rigid officialism breaks in upon the voluntary compromises of the home, that officialism itself will be only rigid in its action and will be exceedingly limp in its thought. Intellectually it will be at least as vague as the amateur arrangements of the home, and the only difference is that the domestic arrangements are in the only real sense practical; that is, they are founded on experiences that have been suffered. The others are what is now generally called scientific; that is, they are founded on experiments that have not yet been made. As a matter of fact, instead of invading the family with the blundering bureaucracy that mismanages the public services, it would be far more philosophical to work the reform the other way round. It would be really quite as reasonable to alter the laws of the nation so as to resemble the laws of the nursery. The punishments would be far less horrible, far more humorous, and far more really calculated to make men feel they had made fools of themselves. It would be a pleasant change if a judge, instead of putting on the black cap, had to put on the dunce's cap; or if we could stand a financier in his own corner.

Of course this opinion is rare, and reactionary—whatever that may mean. Modern education is founded on the principle that a parent is more likely to be cruel than anybody else. It passes over the obvious fact that he is *less* likely to be cruel than anybody else. Anybody may happen to be cruel; but the first chances of cruelty come with the whole colourless and indifferent crowd of total strangers and mechanical mercenaries, whom it is now the custom to call in as infallible agents of improvement; policemen, doctors, detectives, inspectors, instructors, and so on. They are automatically given arbitrary power because there are here and there such things as criminal parents; as if there were no such things as criminal doctors or criminal school-masters. A mother is not always judicious about her child's diet; so it is given into the control of Dr. Crippen.[1] A father is thought not to teach his sons the purest morality; so they are put under the tutorship of Eugene Aram.[2] These celebrated criminals are no more rare in

[1] Hawley Harvey Crippen (1861–1910) was an American doctor who was also a murderer.

[2] Eugene Aram (1704–1759) was an English schoolmaster who was also a murderer.

their respective professions than the cruel parents are in the profession of parenthood. But indeed the case is far stronger than this; and there is no need to rely on the case of such criminals at all. The ordinary weaknesses of human nature will explain all the weaknesses of bureaucracy and business government all over the world. The official need only be an ordinary man to be more indifferent to other people's children than to his own; and even to sacrifice other people's family prosperity to his own. He may be bored; he may be bribed; he may be brutal, for any one of the thousand reasons that ever made a man a brute. All this elementary common sense is entirely left out of account in our educational and social systems of today. It is assumed that the hireling will *not* flee, and that solely because he is a hireling. It is denied that the shepherd will lay down his life for the sheep; or for that matter, even that the she-wolf will fight for the cubs. We are to believe that mothers are inhuman; but not that officials are human. There are unnatural parents, but there are no natural passions; at least, there are none where the fury of King Lear dared to find them—in the beadle. Such is the latest light on the education of the young; and the same principle that is applied to the child is applied to the husband and wife. Just as it assumes that a child will certainly be loved by anybody except his mother, so it assumes that a man can be happy with anybody except the one woman he has himself chosen for his wife.

Thus the coercive spirit of the state prevails over the free promise of the family, in the shape of formal officialism. But this is not the most coercive of the coercive elements in the modern commonwealth. An even more rigid and ruthless external power is that of industrial employment and unemployment. An even more ferocious enemy of the family is the factory. Between these modern mechanical things the ancient natural institution is not being reformed or modified or even cut down; it is being torn in pieces. It is not being torn in pieces in the sense of a true metaphor, like a thing caught in a hideous clockwork of manufacture. It is literally torn in pieces, in that the husband may go to one factory, the wife to another, and the child to a third. Each will become the servant of a separate financial group, which is more and more gaining the political power of a feudal group. But whereas feudalism received the loyalty of families, the lords of the new servile state win receive only the loyalty of individuals; that is, of lonely men and even of lost children.

It is sometimes said that Socialism attacks the family; which is founded on little beyond the accident that some Socialists believe in free-love. I have been a Socialist, and I am no longer a Socialist, and at no time did I believe in free-love. It is true, I think in a large and unconscious sense, that State Socialism encourages the general coercive claim I have been considering. But if it be true that Socialism attacks the family in theory, it is far more certain that Capitalism attacks it in practice. It is a paradox, but a plain fact, that men never notice a thing as long as it exists in practice. Men who will note a heresy will ignore an abuse. Let any one who doubts the paradox imagine the newspapers formally printing along with the Honours' List a price list, for peerages and knighthoods; though everybody knows they are bought and sold. So the factory is destroying the family in fact; and need depend on no poor mad theorist who dreams of destroying it in fancy. And what is destroying it is nothing so plausible as free-love; but something rather to be described as an enforced fear. It is economic punishment more terrible than legal punishment, which may yet land us in slavery as the only safety.

From its first days in the forest this human group had to fight against wild monsters; and so it is now fighting against these wild machines. It only managed to survive then, and it will only manage to survive now, by a strong internal sanctity; a tacit oath or dedication deeper than that of the city or the tribe. But though this silent promise was always present, it took at a certain turning point of our history a special form which I shall try to sketch in the next chapter. That turning point was the creation of Christendom by the religion which created it. Nothing will destroy the sacred triangle; and even the Christian faith, the most amazing revolution that ever took place in the mind, served only in a sense to turn that triangle upside down. It held up a mystical mirror in which the order of the three things was reversed; and added a holy family of child, mother and father to the human family of father, mother and child.

On Certain Modern Writers and the Institution of the Family*

The family may fairly be considered, one would think, an ultimate human institution. Every one would admit that it has been the main cell and central unit of almost all societies hitherto, except, indeed, such societies as that of Lacedaemon, which went in for "efficiency," and has, therefore, perished, and left not a trace behind. Christianity, even enormous as was its revolution, did not alter this ancient and savage sanctity; it merely reversed it. It did not deny the trinity of father, mother, and child. It merely read

---

*"On Certain Modern Writers and the Institution of the Family", *Heretics*, in *CW* I 136–45.

it backwards, making it run child, mother, father. This it called, not the family, but the Holy Family, for many things are made holy by being turned upside down. But some sages of our own decadence have made a serious attack on the family. They have impugned it, as I think wrongly; and its defenders have defended it, and defended it wrongly. The common defence of the family is that, amid the stress and fickleness of life, it is peaceful, pleasant, and at one. But there is another defence of the family which is possible, and to me evident; this defence is that the family is not peaceful and not pleasant and not at one.

It is not fashionable to say much nowadays of the advantages of the small community. We are told that we must go in for large empires and large ideas. There is one advantage, however, in the small state, the city, or the village, which only the wilfully blind can overlook. The man who lives in a small community lives in a much larger world. He knows much more of the fierce varieties and uncompromising divergences of men. The reason is obvious. In a large community we can choose our companions. In a small community our companions are chosen for us. Thus in all extensive and highly civilized societies groups come into existence founded upon what is called sympathy, and shut out the real world more sharply than the gates of a monastery. There is nothing really narrow about the clan; the thing which is really narrow is the clique. The men of the clan live together because they all wear the same tartan or are all descended from the same sacred cow; but in their souls, by the divine luck of things, there will always be more colours than in any tartan. But the men of the clique live together because they have the same kind of soul, and their narrowness is a narrowness of spiritual coherence and contentment, like that which exists in hell. A big society exists in order to form cliques. A big society is a society for the promotion of narrowness. It is a machinery for the purpose of guarding the solitary and sensitive individual from all experience of the bitter and bracing human compromises. It is, in the most literal sense of the words, a society for the prevention of Christian knowledge.

We can see this change, for instance, in the modern transformation of the thing called a club. When London was smaller, and the parts of London more self-contained and parochial, the club was what it still is in villages, the opposite of what it is now in great cities. Then the club was valued as a place where a man could be sociable. Now the club is valued as a place where a man can be unsociable. The more the enlargement and elaboration of our civilization goes on the more the club ceases to be a place where a man can have a noisy argument, and becomes more and more a place where a man can have what is somewhat fantastically called a quiet chop. Its aim is to make a man comfortable, and to make a man comfortable is to make him the opposite of sociable. Sociability, like all good things, is full of discomforts, dangers, and renunciations. The club tends to produce the most degraded of all combinations—the luxurious anchorite, the man who combines the self-indulgence of Lucullus with the insane loneliness of St. Simeon Stylites.

If we were to-morrow morning snowed up in the street in which we live, we should step suddenly into a much larger and much wilder world than we have ever known. And it is the whole effort of the typically modern person to escape from the street in which he lives. First he invents modern hygiene and goes to Margate. Then he invents modern culture and goes to Florence. Then he invents modern imperialism and goes to Timbuctoo. He goes to the fantastic borders of the earth. He pretends to shoot tigers. He almost rides on a camel. And in all this he

is still essentially fleeing from the street in which he was
born; and of this flight he is always ready with his own
explanation. He says he is fleeing from his street because
it is dull; he is lying. He is really fleeing from his street
because it is a great deal too exciting. It is exciting because
it is exacting; it is exacting because it is alive. He can visit
Venice because to him the Venetians are only Venetians;
the people in his own street are men. He can stare at the
Chinese because for him the Chinese are a passive thing to
be stared at; if he stares at the old lady in the next garden,
she becomes active. He is forced to flee, in short, from the
too stimulating society of his equals—of free men, perverse, personal, deliberately different from himself. The
street in Brixton is too glowing and overpowering. He
has to soothe and quiet himself among tigers and vultures,
camels and crocodiles. These creatures are indeed very different from himself. But they do not put their shape or
colour or custom into a decisive intellectual competition
with his own. They do not seek to destroy his principles
and assert their own; the stranger monsters of the suburban
street do seek to do this. The camel does not contort his
features into a fine sneer because Mr. Robinson has not
got a hump; the cultured gentleman at No. 5 does exhibit
a sneer because Robinson has not got a dado. The vulture
will not roar with laughter because a man does not fly;
but the major at No. 9 will roar with laughter because
a man does not smoke. The complaint we commonly
have to make of our neighbours is that they will not, as
we express it, mind their own business. We do not really
mean that they will not mind their own business. If our
neighbours did not mind their own business they would
be asked abruptly for their rent, and would rapidly cease
to be our neighbours. What we really mean when we say
that they cannot mind their own business is something

much deeper. We do not dislike them because they have so little force and fire that they cannot be interested in themselves. We dislike them because they have so much force and fire that they can be interested in us as well. What we dread about our neighbours, in short, is not the narrowness of their horizon, but their superb tendency to broaden it. And all aversions to ordinary humanity have this general character. They are not aversions to its feebleness (as is pretended), but to its energy. The misanthropes pretend that they despise humanity for its weakness. As a matter of fact, they hate it for its strength.

Of course, this shrinking from the brutal vivacity and brutal variety of common men is a perfectly reasonable and excusable thing as long as it does not pretend to any point of superiority. It is when it calls itself aristocracy or aestheticism or a superiority to the bourgeoisie that its inherent weakness has in justice to be pointed out. Fastidiousness is the most pardonable of vices; but it is the most unpardonable of virtues. Nietzsche, who represents most prominently this pretentious claim of the fastidious, has a description somewhere—a very powerful description in the purely literary sense—of the disgust and disdain which consume him at the sight of the common people with their common faces, their common voices, and their common minds. As I have said, this attitude is almost beautiful if we may regard it as pathetic. Nietzsche's aristocracy has about it all the sacredness that belongs to the weak. When he makes us feel that he cannot endure the innumerable faces, the incessant voices, the overpowering omnipresence which belongs to the mob, he will have the sympathy of anybody who has ever been sick on a steamer or tired in a crowded omnibus. Every man has hated mankind when he was less than a man. Every man has had humanity in his eyes like a blinding fog, humanity in his nostrils like a suffocating smell. But when Nietzsche has the incredible lack of humour and lack of imagination to ask us to believe that his aristocracy is an aristocracy of strong muscles or an aristocracy of strong wills, it is necessary to point out the truth. It is an aristocracy of weak nerves.

We make our friends; we make our enemies; but God makes our next-door neighbour. Hence he comes to us clad in all the careless terrors of nature; he is as strange as the stars, as reckless and indifferent as the rain. He is Man, the most terrible of the beasts. That is why the old religions and the old scriptural language showed so sharp a wisdom when they spoke, not of one's duty towards humanity, but one's duty towards one's neighbour. The duty towards humanity may often take the form of some choice which is personal or even pleasurable. That duty may be a hobby; it may even be a dissipation. We may work in the East End because we are peculiarly fitted to work in the East End, or because we think we are; we may fight for the cause of international peace because we are very fond of fighting. The most monstrous martyrdom, the most repulsive experience, may be the result of choice or a kind of taste. We may be so made as to be particularly fond of lunatics or specially interested in leprosy. We may love negroes because they are black or German Socialists because they are pedantic. But we have to love our neighbour because he is there—a much more alarming reason for a much more serious operation. He is the sample of humanity which is actually given us. Precisely because he may be anybody he is everybody. He is a symbol because he is an accident.

Doubtless men flee from small environments into lands that are very deadly. But this is natural enough; for they are not fleeing from death. They are fleeing from life. And this principle applies to ring within ring of the social system of humanity. It is perfectly reasonable that men should seek for some particular variety of the human type, so long as they are seeking for that variety of the human type, and not for mere human variety. It is quite proper that a British diplomatist should seek the society of Japanese generals, if what he wants is Japanese generals. But if what he wants is people different from himself, he had much better stop at home and discuss religion with the housemaid. It is quite reasonable that the village genius should come up to conquer London if what he wants is to conquer London. But if he wants to conquer something fundamentally and symbolically hostile and also very strong, he had much better remain where he is and have a row with the rector. The man in the suburban street is quite right if he goes to Ramsgate for the sake of Ramsgate—a difficult thing to imagine. But if, as he expresses it, he goes to Ramsgate "for a change," then he would have a much more romantic and even melodramatic change if he jumped over the wall into his neighbour's garden. The consequences would be bracing in a sense far beyond the possibilities of Ramsgate hygiene.

Now, exactly as this principle applies to the empire, to the nation within the empire, to the city within the nation, to the street within the city, so it applies to the home within the street. The institution of the family is to be commended for precisely the same reasons that the institution of the nation, or the institution of the city, are in this matter to be commended. It is a good thing for a man to live in a family for the same reason that it is a good thing for a man to be besieged in a city. It is a good thing for a man to live in a family in the same sense that it is a beautiful and delightful thing for a man to be snowed up in a street. They all force him to realize that life is not a thing from outside, but a thing from inside. Above all, they all insist upon the fact that life, if it be a truly stimulating and fascinating life, is a thing which, of its nature, exists in spite of ourselves. The modern writers who have suggested, in a more or less open manner, that the family is a bad institution, have generally confined themselves to suggesting, with much sharpness, bitterness, or pathos, that perhaps the family is not always very congenial. Of course the family is a good institution because it is uncongenial. It is wholesome precisely because it contains so many divergencies and varieties. It is, as the sentimentalists say, like a little kingdom, and, like most other little kingdoms, is generally in a state of something resembling anarchy. It is exactly because our brother George is not interested in our religious difficulties, but is interested in the Trocadero Restaurant, that the family has some of the bracing qualities of the commonwealth. It is precisely because our uncle Henry does not approve of the theatrical ambitions of our sister Sarah that the family is like humanity. The men and women who, for good reasons and bad, revolt against the family, are, for good reasons and bad, simply revolting against mankind. Aunt Elizabeth is unreasonable, like mankind. Papa is excitable, like mankind. Our youngest brother is mischievous, like mankind. Grandpapa is stupid, like the world; he is old, like the world.

Those who wish, rightly or wrongly, to step out of all this, do definitely wish to step into a narrower world. They are dismayed and terrified by the largeness and variety of the family. Sarah wishes to find a world wholly consisting of private theatricals; George wishes to think the Trocadero a cosmos. I do not say, for a moment, that the flight to this narrower life may not be the right thing for the individual, any more than I say the same thing about flight into a monastery. But I do say that anything is bad and artificial which tends to make these people succumb to the strange delusion that they are stepping into a world which is actually larger and more varied than their own. The best way that a man could test his readiness to encounter the common variety of mankind would be to climb down a chimney into any house at random, and get on as well as possible with the people inside. And that is essentially what each one of us did on the day that he was born.

This is, indeed, the sublime and special romance of the family. It is romantic because it is a toss-up. It is romantic because it is everything that its enemies call it. It is romantic because it is arbitrary. It is romantic because it is there. So long as you have groups of men chosen rationally, you have some special or sectarian atmosphere. It is when you have groups of men chosen irrationally that you have men. The element of adventure begins to exist; for an adventure is, by its nature, a thing that comes to us. It is a thing that chooses us, not a thing that we choose. Falling in love has been often regarded as the supreme adventure, the supreme romantic accident. In so much as there is in it something outside ourselves, something of a sort of merry fatalism, this is very true. Love does take us and transfigure and torture us. It does break our hearts with an unbearable beauty, like the unbearable beauty of music. But in so far as we have certainly something to do with the matter; in so far as we are in some sense prepared to fall in love and in some sense jump into it; in so far as we do to some extent choose and to some extent even judge—in all this falling in love is not truly romantic, is not truly adventurous at all. In this degree the supreme adventure is not falling in love. The supreme adventure is being born. There we do walk suddenly into a splendid and startling trap. There we do see something of which we have not dreamed before. Our father and mother do lie in wait for us and leap out on us, like brigands from a bush. Our uncle is a surprise. Our aunt is, in the beautiful common expression, a bolt from the blue. When we step into the family, by the act of being born, we do step into a world which is incalculable, into a world which has its own strange laws, into a world which could do without us, into a world that we have not made. In other words, when we step into the family we step into a fairy-tale.

This colour as of a fantastic narrative ought to cling to the family and to our relations with it throughout life. Romance is the deepest thing in life; romance is deeper even than reality. For even if reality could be proved to be misleading, it still could not be proved to be unimportant or unimpressive. Even if the facts are false, they are still very strange. And this strangeness of life, this unexpected and even perverse element of things as they fall out, remains incurably interesting. The circumstances we can regulate may become tame or pessimistic; but the "circumstances over which we have no control" remain god-like to those who, like Mr. Micawber, can call on them and renew their strength. People wonder why the novel is the most popular form of literature; people wonder why it is read more than books of science or books of metaphysics. The reason is very simple; it is merely that the novel is more true than they are. Life may sometimes legitimately appear as a book of science. Life may sometimes appear, and with a much greater legitimacy, as a book of metaphysics. But life is always a novel. Our existence may cease to be a song; it may cease even to be a beautiful lament. Our existence may not be an intelligible justice, or even a recognizable wrong. But our existence is still a story. In the fiery alphabet of every sunset is written, "to be continued in our next." If we have sufficient intellect, we can finish a philosophical and exact deduction, and be certain that we are finishing it right. With the adequate brain-power we could finish any scientific discovery, and be certain that we were finishing it right. But not with the most gigantic intellect could we finish the simplest or silliest story, and be certain that we were finishing it right. That is because a story has behind it, not merely intellect which is partly mechanical, but will, which is in its essence divine. The narrative writer can send his hero to the gallows if he likes in the last chapter but one. He can do it by the same divine caprice whereby he, the author, can go to the gallows himself, and to hell afterwards if he chooses. And the same civilization, the chivalric European civilization which asserted free-will in the thirteenth century, produced the thing called "fiction" in the eighteenth. When Thomas Aquinas asserted the spiritual liberty of man, he created all the bad novels in the circulating libraries.

But in order that life should be a story or romance to us, it is necessary that a great part of it, at any rate, should be settled for us without our permission. If we wish life to be a system, this may be a nuisance; but if we wish it to be a drama, it is an essential. It may often happen, no doubt, that a drama may be written by somebody else which we like very little. But we should like it still less if the author came before the curtain every hour or so, and forced on us the whole trouble of inventing the next act. A man has control over many things in his life; he has control over enough things to be the hero of a novel. But if he had control over everything, there would be so much hero that there would be no novel. And the reason why the lives of the rich are at bottom so tame and uneventful is simply that they can choose the events. They are dull because they are omnipotent. They fail to feel adventures because they can make the adventures. The thing which keeps life romantic and full of fiery possibilities is the existence of these great plain limitations which force all of us to meet the things we do not like or do not expect. It is vain for the supercilious moderns to talk of being in uncongenial surroundings. To be in a romance is to be in uncongenial surroundings. To be born into this earth is to be born into uncongenial surroundings, hence to be born into a romance. Of all these great limitations and frameworks which fashion and create the poetry and variety of life, the family is the most definite and important. Hence it is misunderstood by the moderns, who imagine that romance would exist most perfectly in a complete state of what they call liberty. They think that if a man makes a gesture it would be a startling and romantic matter that the sun should fall from the sky. But the startling and romantic thing about the sun is that it does not fall from the sky. They are seeking under every shape and form a world where there are no limitations—that is, a world where there are no outlines; that is, a world where there are no shapes. There is nothing baser than that infinity. They say they wish to be as strong as the universe, but they really wish the whole universe as weak as themselves.

What Is the Institution of the Family?*

It is a strange thing that people seem to have forgotten what is meant by an institution; at the very moment when they are instituting any number of new institutions which never had so much popular support or moral authority as the old institutions. Officialism is perpetually splitting up into "new departments," without even telling us of what they are supposed to be a part. There are not only more and more bureaucrats, but more and more bureaus. Every

*Excerpt was originally published in *Illustrated London News*, October 13, 1934.

week or so a new law that we never heard of gives arbitrary powers to a man whom nobody has ever heard of. Powers of action, not demanded from below, but only delegated from above, cover the nation like a network as tight and as thin as wire. And yet, amidst all this officialism, people seem to have forgotten the original meaning of an office. Amid all this intensified institutionalism, they cannot grasp what goes along with the very nature of an institution. We see this with astonishing vividness in the debates about the institution of Marriage; or about the Family, which is not only an institution, but a foundation, the foundation of nearly all institutions.

We have all heard well-intentioned but somewhat bewildered people say something like this: "Of course, we all feel there is something truly sacred about the ideal of true Marriage; but the sacredness consists in the presence of Love; and when that lessens or changes or is interrupted for any reason, then the true marriage is no longer there at all, and its sanctity has departed." Now nobody talks in this way about any other ideal that is expressed in any other institution. Of course, in one sense it is true enough; for the idea is more than the institution. But if it is identified with moods and changes of feeling, it cannot possibly be expressed in any institution at all. Even the newest nine-hundred-and-ninety-ninth sub-division and additional branch of the Ministry of Breathing Exercises must be based on the notion that somebody is supposed to look after something, even when he is feeling bored with it. Even the Committee on Compulsory Dentistry for the Dogs of the Unemployed (appointed by the schedule of an Act of Parliament passed without debate in a House containing six members), even that large-minded body must distinguish between those who are members and those who are not, and must continue to make itself a nuisance to everybody else, even if all its members are a nuisance to each other. These earnest and ethical social workers must, after all, do some work; even if they hate their jobs as much as we hate their faces. And if this is true even of the crudest and most experimental of minor institutions, it is obviously much more true of those other elementary and essential institutions of which the Family was originally supposed to be one. The most obvious examples are the institution of Private Property and the institution of Public Order; which we call the Government or the State. When a man does not believe in the institution of Private Property, as understood by the old Capitalists, he generally does believe all the more absolutely (we might say abjectly) in the institution called the State, as worshipped by the Socialists and Communists; or, for that matter, by a good many of the Fascists or the Hitlerites. Under these two or three streams of tendency (as Matthew Arnold would say), the other institution called the Family has almost been washed away; but chiefly because it is the subject of this sort of washy sentiment.

For nobody dreams of applying that sort of washy sentiment to any of the other institutions. Nobody says that, so long as the sight of the policeman at the corner of the street still thrills me like the sight of a soldier watching, sword in hand, over the fatherland, so long and no longer I may tolerate the policeman and allow him to regulate the traffic; but if, in some empty and dreary hour, I grow cold towards the policeman, I feel no gush of inspiration at the sight of his boots, I even feel suddenly (with the hideous stab of some highly modern poem) that I do not like his face—then, all is over between me and the policeman; I no longer recognise his function in the State; I become a philosophic anarchist and he becomes an unintelligible tyrant. Nobody says this; for the obvious reason that

Government or the State would never have existed at all, for forty-eight hours, if it was dissolved by any change of emotion or the momentary loss of our purely imaginative appreciation of its value. It is the same with the balancing institution of Private Property. Government does exist for the ultimate purpose of giving us a feeling of security; property does exist for the ultimate purpose of giving us a feeling of personal dignity; and marriage does exist for the ultimate purpose of giving us a feeling of happiness, mainly founded on affection. But none of them would exist, or would ever have existed, if there had not been some rule of fidelity and continuity, that could be counted on to rise superior to mere moods and emotions. I like my walking-stick; but I do not like the philosopher who tells me it is only my walking-stick while I am thinking about it. Suppose I am proud and sensitive on the subject of my cucumber-frame (which no one who knows me will believe), and that I take an intermittent but intense delight in the fact that Mr. Robinson, next door, also regards it with admiration, though mine is the admiration of possession and his is the admiration of envy. I really cannot listen to the theory that the cucumber-frame gradually comes to belong to Mr. Robinson, as my moments of admiration become more intermittent, and his more intense or more frequent. I cannot accept the view that he gradually grows to be the possessor of my garden, because he lies awake at night thinking about my garden, when I am forced to think about something else; such as the horrid necessity of writing articles for the Press. In short, Private Property may be a bad institution, as the Communists think; or it may be a good institution, as I think. But it cannot be an institution at all unless it is to some extent a fixture removed from the fluctuation of Mr. Robinson's feelings and mine.

The Family is the only institution that is discussed in this senseless sentimental fashion; and, therefore, the Family is the only institution that has very nearly ceased to exist. Those other institutions, those much more official, oppressive, and even tyrannical institutions, do continue to exist. And that is because they have laws and loyalties that are supposed to survive changes of sentiment. The two chief things that prevail in the modern world are the State and that Big Business that is bigger than the State. Neither of those two things excuses a man because of a change in his emotions. He is under the King's Government a long time after that high moment of historical enthusiasm when he really felt a romantic loyalty to the King. He has to "clock-in" at the Cosmopolis Cotton Works long after that brief dream of youthful ambition when he thought he would some day be manager. In short, the other institutions do still demand, in a more modern and therefore a more vulgar form, something analogous to the old idea of a vow. People do at least sign on "for the duration of the war."

Now the Family is by far the freest of such groups, and the chief prop of freedom. It is the small human group, in which the individual counts, as he cannot count in the State or the Trust. It is the only human government that permits a sense of humour; because it is the only form that is familiar with the personalities of its subjects. It is also the only human group that is at first an association of volunteers. That is, its origin is in a voluntary avowal and acceptance; whereas we are all born subjects to some Government; and most of us, nowadays, are economically driven to be the servants of some Trust. In every way this institution, as compared with other institutions, is a thing of life and liberty. But it cannot endure, if it is not a thing of loyalty and continuity. As things look at present, it will be swallowed by the State or the Trust, or both; and most of its humble but healthy representatives will not know which is which.

The Alternative to the Family[*]

Nothing strikes me more about the modern drift from domesticity than the fact that it is really only a drift, and not even a drive; that it consists of people following a fashion rather than a heresy; that is, of each person acting not because he is individually convinced, but because he is collectively influenced. The sheep do not follow even a wicked shepherd; the sheep simply follow each other. We know, of course, that there has been a certain parade of originality and ethical defiance in the limited number of sheep who really like showing off. But we have really had very little of the real evil intentions of the wolf in sheep's clothing. What we have had is the pathetic masquerade of the sheep in wolf's clothing. We have seen the sort of suburban intellectual, who dare not fail to catch his train or to keep his job, going off and masquerading in plays and books as a man ready to murder his wife as a protest against marriage, or his mother as a protest against life. We have seen a great deal of the sham wolf; who is quite different from the sham sheep. But neither one nor the other has really been able to throw off the oppression of mere modern fashions and fads. . . .

For, after all, in almost all these current controversies, it is true to say that nobody has really discussed *the alternative* to the Family. The only obvious alternative is the State. Even supposing that the extreme anarchist school could prevail in a sort of universal riot of promiscuity, the result could only

[*] Excerpt was originally published in *Illustrated London News*, January 4, 1936.

be that the whole new generation of humanity would be thrown on the resources of the only thing which would be considered responsible for them.... For, given any freedom of that sort, the State does become one vast Foundling Hospital. If families will not be responsible for their own children then officials will be responsible for other people's children. The care of all such things will pass into their hands; because there will be nobody else to notice such a trifle as a living soul born alive into the world. The total control of human life will pass to the State; and it will be a very totalitarian State. I know there are some who maintain that paid officials will be more devoted than parents; but it is very hard to see on what this can be based, unless it is the pay. Yet there is the whole world, and rather especially the whole modern world, to attest that those who are well paid can be badly bored. Those who imagine that they could not be bored with babies do not know much about babies. We always come back to the unanswerable argument of nature; that there do happen to be one or two persons who are less bored with one particular very boring baby than everyone else would be. That common sense is the concrete foundation of the family; and no negative reaction against it comes anywhere near to having a positive substitute for it. Those who have a vague idea that educationists could take it in turns or experts divide the baby between them, are simply people who suppose that there can be twenty officials to one citizen. A baby cannot be divided to any general social satisfaction, as Solomon discovered some time ago [see I Kings 3:16–27]; and the person who least desires to see it divided will still be the person most likely to take it on as a whole, and as a whole-time job.

2

Love … and Sex

The Strange Music

Other loves may sink and settle, other loves may
loose and slack,
But I wander like a minstrel with a harp upon his
back,
Though the harp be on my bosom, though I finger
and I fret,
Still, my hope is all before me: for I cannot play it
yet.

In your strings is hid a music that no hand hath e'er
let fall,
In your soul is sealed a pleasure that you have not
known at all;
Pleasure subtle as your spirit, strange and slender as
your frame,
Fiercer than the pain that folds you, softer than
your sorrow's name.

Not as mine, my soul's anointed, not as mine the
rude and light
Easy mirth of many faces, swaggering pride of song
and fight;
Something stranger, something sweeter, something
waiting you afar,
Secret as your stricken senses, magic as your sorrows
are.

But on this, God's harp supernal, stretched but to
  be stricken once,
Hoary time is a beginner, Life a bungler, Death a
  dunce.
But I will not fear to match them—no, by God, I
  will not fear,
I will learn you, I will play you and the stars stand
  still to hear.

We have the only civilization that is founded on first
love, on the single and romantic view of sex; we have the
only scheme that believes in chivalry; we alone serve St.
George and St. Valentine.

— *Daily News*, May 23, 1903

A perfectly rational lover would never get married.... A
perfectly rational army would run away.

— "The Dramatist", *George Bernard Shaw*

Some say the poor should give up having children, which
means they should give up the great virtue of sexual sanity.

— "Dickens and Christmas", *Charles Dickens*

Love is the most realistic thing in the world.

— "The Great Victorian Poets", *The Victorian Age*

It is a very queer feature of current poetry that there is
hardly anywhere such a thing as a love poem. The poetry
is about something that they call sex.

— *Illustrated London News*, August 19, 1933

Sex is quite different from anything else in the world.

— "The Suffragist", *A Miscellany of Men*

About sex especially men are born unbalanced; we might almost say men are born mad. They scarcely reach sanity till they reach sanctity.

> — "The Demons and the Philosophers",
> *The Everlasting Man*

The two first facts which a healthy boy or girl feels about sex are these: first that it is beautiful and then that it is dangerous.... All people have an absolutely clean instinct in the matter. Mankind declares with one deafening voice: that sex may be ecstatic so long as it is also restricted. It is not necessary that the restriction should be reasonable; it is only necessary that it should restrict. That is the beginning of all purity; and purity is the beginning of all passion. In other words, the creation of conditions for love, or even for flirting, is common-sense.

> — *Illustrated London News*, January 9, 1909

Sex and breathing are about the only two things that generally work best when they are least worried about.

> — "The Suffragist", *A Miscellany of Men*

The more the sexes are in violent contrast the less likely they are to be in violent collision.

> — "The Sectarian of Society",
> *A Miscellany of Men*

The human race has always admired the Catholic virtues, however little it can practise them; and oddly enough it has admired most those of them the modern world most sharply disputes.

> — "An Interlude of Argument",
> *The Ball and the Cross*

There is a right relation of the sexes; there is a right rule about it; and there is a wrong appeal calculated to encourage a wrong relation.

— *Illustrated London News*,
March 23, 1929

The heretics who defend sexual manias will never admit that they are anything but chaste.

— *Daily News*, September 5, 1904

The exaggeration of sex becomes sexlessness. It becomes something that is much worse than mere anarchy, something that can truly be described as malice; a war, not against the restraints required by virtue but against virtue itself. The old moral theology called it malice; and there will be no future for the modern psychology until it again studies the old moral theology. Sex is the bait and not the hook; but in that last extreme of evil the man likes the hook and not the bait.

— *Illustrated London News*,
March 30, 1929

The ordinary argument that sex can be treated calmly and freely like anything else is the most loathsome cant in this canting epoch.

— *Daily News*, February 19, 1910

The moment sex ceases to be a servant it becomes a tyrant.

— "The World St. Francis Found", *St. Francis of Assisi*

The frightful punishment of mere sex emancipation is not anarchy but bureaucracy.

— *Illustrated London News*, January 4, 1936

Most of the current ideas on all these matters of sexual dignity and sexual difference seem to be in an almost unlimited chaos.

— *New Witness*,
May 26, 1922

The sacramental idea of sex is much less understood than it was centuries before, and probably much less than it will be centuries after.

— *Illustrated London News*,
August 15, 1931

The same age which tends to economic slavery tends to social anarchy; and especially to sexual anarchy. So long as men can be driven in droves like sheep, they can be as promiscuous as sheep.

— *G. K.'s Weekly*,
March 9, 1929

Sex is not a thing like eating and sleeping. There is something dangerous and disproportionate in its place in human nature, for whatever reason; and it does really need a special purification and dedication. ... If sex is treated merely as one innocent natural thing among others, what happens is that every other innocent natural thing becomes soaked and sodden with sex.

— "The World St. Francis Found",
St. Francis of Assisi

Though a proper Noah's Ark should contain two specimens of every animal, nobody ever proposed that it should contain two Noahs.

— *Illustrated London News*,
July 2, 1921

To Frances[*]

I am looking over the sea and endeavouring to reckon up the estate I have to offer you. As far as I can make out my equipment for starting on a journey to fairyland consists of the following items.

1st. A Straw Hat. The oldest part of this admirable relic shows traces of pure Norman work. The vandalism of Cromwell's soldiers has left us little of the original hat-band.

2nd. A Walking Stick, very knobby and heavy: admirably fitted to break the head of any denizen of Suffolk who denies that you are the noblest of ladies, but of no other manifest use.

3rd. A copy of Walt Whitman's poems, once nearly given to Salter, but quite forgotten. It has his name in it still with an affectionate inscription from his sincere friend Gilbert Chesterton. I wonder if he will ever have it.

4th. A number of letters from a young lady, containing everything good and generous and loyal and holy and wise that isn't in Walt Whitman's poems.

5th. An unwieldy sort of a pocket knife, the blades mostly having an edge of a more varied and picturesque outline than is provided by the prosaic cutter. The chief element however is a thing "to take stones out of a horse's hoof." What a beautiful sensation of security it gives one to reflect that if one should ever have money enough to buy a horse and should happen to buy one and the horse should happen to have a stone in his hoof—that one is ready; one stands prepared, with a defiant smile!

[*] Excerpt is from a letter to his fiancee, Frances Blogg, in *Gilbert Keith Chesterton*, ed. Maisie Ward (New York: Sheed and Ward, 1943), pp. 94–96, 98–102, 104–5.

6th. Passing from the last miracle of practical foresight, we come to a box of matches. Every now and then I strike one of these, because fire is beautiful and burns your fingers. Some people think this a waste of matches: the same people who object to the building of Cathedrals.

7th. About three pounds in gold and silver, the remains of one of Mr. Unwin's bursts of affection: those explosions of spontaneous love for myself, which, such is the perfect order and harmony of his mind, occur at startlingly exact intervals of time.

8th. A book of Children's Rhymes, in manuscript, called the "Weather Book" [*Greybeards at Play*, Chesterton's first book] about finished, and destined for Mr. Nutt. I have been working at it fairly steadily, which I think jolly creditable under the circumstances. One can't put anything interesting in it. They'll understand those things when they grow up.

9th. A tennis racket—nay, start not. It is a part of the new régime, and the only new and neat-looking thing in the Museum. We'll soon mellow it—like the straw hat. My brother and I are teaching each other lawn tennis.

10th. A soul, hitherto idle and omnivorous but now happy enough to be ashamed of itself.

11th. A body, equally idle and quite equally omnivorous, absorbing tea, coffee, claret, sea-water and oxygen to its own perfect satisfaction. It is happiest swimming, I think, the sea being about a convenient size.

12th. A Heart—mislaid somewhere. And that is about all the property of which an inventory can be made at present. After all, my tastes are stoically simple. A straw hat, a stick, a box of matches and some of his own poetry. What more does man require? ...

When we set up a house, darling (honeysuckle porch, yew clipt hedge, bees, poetry and eight shillings a week),

I think you will have to do the shopping. There was a great and glorious man who said, "Give us the luxuries of life and we will dispense with the necessities." That I think would be a splendid motto to write (in letters of brown gold) over the porch of our hypothetical home. There will be a sofa for you, for example, but no chairs, for I prefer the floor. There will be a select store of chocolate-creams and the rest will be bread and water. We will each retain a suit of evening dress for great occasions, and at other times clothe ourselves in the skins of wild beasts (how pretty you would look) which would fit your taste in furs and be economical.

I have sometimes thought it would be very fine to take an ordinary house, a very poor, commonplace house in West Kensington, say, and make it symbolic. Not artistic—Heaven—O Heaven forbid. My blood boils when I think of the affronts put by knock-kneed pictorial epicures on the strong, honest, ugly, patient shapes of necessary things: the brave old bones of life. There are aesthetic pottering prigs who can look on a saucepan without one tear of joy or sadness: mongrel decadents that can see no dignity in the honourable scars of a kettle. So they concentrate all their house decoration on coloured windows that nobody looks out of, and vases of lilies that everybody wishes out of the way. No: my idea (which is much cheaper) is to make a house really allegoric: really explain its own essential meaning. Mystical or ancient sayings should be inscribed on every object, the more prosaic the object the better; and the more coarsely and rudely the inscription was traced the better. "Hast thou sent the Rain upon the Earth?" [Job 5:10] should be inscribed on the Umbrella-stand: perhaps on the Umbrella. "Even the Hairs of your Head are all numbered" [Lk 12:7] would give a tremendous significance to one's hairbrushes: the words about "living water" [Jn 4:10] would reveal the music and sanctity of the sink: while "our God is a consuming Fire" [Heb 12:29] might be written over the kitchen-grate, to assist the mystic musings of the cook—Shall we ever try that experiment, dearest. Perhaps not, for no words would be golden enough for the tools you had to touch: you would be beauty enough for one house. . . .

By all means let us have bad things in our dwelling and make them good things. I shall offer no objection to your having an occasional dragon to dinner, or a penitent Griffin to sleep in the spare bed. The image of you taking a Sunday school of little Devils is pleasing. They will look up, first in savage wonder, then in vague respect; they will see the most glorious and noble lady that ever lived since their prince tempted Eve, with a halo of hair and great heavenly eyes that seem to make the good at the heart of things almost too terribly simple and naked for the sons of flesh: and as they gaze, their tails will drop off, and their wings will sprout: and they will become Angels in six lessons. . . .

I cannot profess to offer any elaborate explanation of your mother's disquiet but I admit it does not wholly surprise me. You see I happen to know one factor in the case, and one only, of which you are wholly ignorant. I know you . . . I know one thing which has made me feel strange before your mother—I know the value of what I take away. I feel (in a weird moment) like the Angel of Death.

You say you want to talk to me about death: my views about death are bright, brisk and entertaining. When Azrael takes a soul it may be to other and brighter worlds: like those whither you and I go together. The transformation called Death may be something as beautiful and dazzling as the transformation called Love. It may make the dead man "happy," just as your mother knows that you are happy. But none the less it is a transformation, and sad sometimes for those left behind. A mother whose child is dying can hardly believe that in the inscrutable Unknown there is anyone who can look to it as well as she. And if a mother cannot trust her child easily to God Almighty, shall I be so mean as to be angry because she cannot trust it easily to me? I tell you I have stood before your mother and felt like a thief. I know you are not going to part: neither physically, mentally, morally nor spiritually. But she sees a new element in your life, wholly from outside—is it not natural, given her temperament, that you should find her perturbed? Oh, dearest, dearest Frances, let us always be very gentle to older people. Indeed, darling, it is not they who are the tyrants, but we. They may interrupt our building in the scaffolding stages: we turn their house upside down when it is their final home and rest. Your mother would certainly have worried if you had been engaged to the Archangel Michael (who, indeed, is bearing his disappointment very well): how much more when you are engaged to an aimless, tactless, reckless, unbrushed, strange-hatted, opinionated scarecrow who has suddenly walked into the vacant place. I could have prophesied her unrest: wait and she will calm down all right, dear. God comfort her: I dare not. . . .

Gilbert Keith Chesterton was born of comfortable but honest parents on the top of Campden Hill, Kensington. He was christened at St. George's Church which stands just under that more imposing building, the Waterworks Tower. This place was chosen, apparently, in order that the whole available water supply might be used in the intrepid attempt to make him a member of Christ, a child of God and an inheritor of the Kingdom of Heaven.

Of the early years of this remarkable man few traces remain. . . . The only really curious thing about his school life was that he had a weird and quite involuntary habit of getting French prizes. They were the only ones he ever got and he never tried to get them. But though the thing was quite mysterious to him, and though he made every effort to avoid it, it went on, being evidently a part of some occult natural law....

Our subject met Lucian Oldershaw. "That night," as Shakespeare says, "there was a star." ... One pleasant Saturday afternoon Lucian said to him, "I am going to take you to see the Bloggs."

"The what?" said the unhappy man.

"The Bloggs," said the other, darkly. Naturally assuming that it was the name of a public-house he reluctantly followed his friend. He came to a small front-garden; if it was a public-house it was not a businesslike one. They raised the latch—they rang the bell. No flower in the pots winked. No brick grinned. No sign in Heaven or earth warned him. The birds sang on in the trees. He went in.

The first time he spent an evening at the Bloggs there was no one there.... But the second time he went there he was plumped down on a sofa beside a being of whom he had a vague impression that brown hair grew at intervals all down her like a caterpillar. Once in the course of conversation she looked straight at him and he said to himself as plainly as if he had read it in a book: "If I had anything to do with this girl I should go on my knees to her: if I spoke with her she would never deceive me: if I depended on her she would never deny me: if I loved her she would never play with me: if I trusted her she would never go back on me: if I remembered her she would never forget me. I may never see her again. Goodbye." It was all said in a flash: but it was all said....

Two years, as they say in the playbills, is supposed to elapse. And here is the subject of this memoir sitting on a balcony above the sea. The time, evening. He is thinking of the whole bewildering record of which the foregoing is a brief outline: he sees how far he has gone wrong and how idle and wasteful and wicked he has often been: how miserably unfitted he is for what he is called upon to be. Let him now declare it and hereafter for ever hold his peace.

But there are four lamps of thanksgiving always before him. The first is for his creation out of the same earth with such a woman as you. The second is that he has not, with all his faults, "gone after strange women." You cannot think how a man's self-restraint is rewarded in this. The third is that he has tried to love everything alive: a dim preparation for loving you. And the fourth is—but no words can express that. Here ends my previous existence. Take it: it led me to you.

Two Stubborn Pieces of Iron[*]

The differences between a man and a woman are at best so obstinate and exasperating that they practically cannot be got over unless there is an atmosphere of exaggerated tenderness and mutual interest. To put the matter in one metaphor, the sexes are two stubborn pieces of iron; if they are to be welded together, it must be while they are red-hot. Every woman has to find out that the husband is a selfish beast, because every man is a selfish beast by the standard of a woman. But let her find out the beast while they are both still in the story of "Beauty and the Beast." Every man has to find out that his wife is cross—that is to say, sensitive to the point of madness; for every woman is

---

[*] Excerpt is from "Two Stubborn Pieces of Iron", in *The Common Man* (New York: Sheed and Ward, 1950), pp. 142–43.

mad by the masculine standard. But let him find out that
she is mad while her madness is more worth considering
than anyone else's sanity.

The Essence of Romance*

All romances consist of three characters.... For the sake
of argument they may be called St. George and the Dragon
and the Princess. In every romance there must be the twin
elements of loving and fighting. In every romance there
must be the three characters: there must be the Princess,
who is a thing to be loved; there must be the Dragon, who
is a thing to be fought; and there must be St. George, who is
a thing that both loves and fights. There have been many
symptoms of cynicism and decay in our modern civilization. But of all the signs of modern feebleness, of lack of
grasp on morals as they actually must be, there has been
none quite so silly or so dangerous as this: that the philosophers of today have started to divide loving from fighting
and to put them into opposite camps.... [But] the two
things imply each other; they implied each other in the
old romance and in the old religion, which were the two
permanent things of humanity. You cannot love a thing
without wanting to fight for it. You cannot fight without
something to fight for. To love a thing without wishing to
fight for it is not love at all; it is lust. It may be an airy, philosophical, and disinterested lust ... but it is lust, because it
is wholly self-indulgent and invites no attack. On the other
hand, fighting for a thing without loving it is not even
fighting; it can only be called a kind of horse-play that is

* Excerpt is from "Nicholas Nickleby", in *Appreciations and Criticisms of the
Works of Charles Dickens*, in *CW*, vol. 15 (San Francisco: Ignatius Press, 1990),
p. 255.

occasionally fatal. Wherever human nature is human and unspoilt by any special sophistry, there exists this natural kinship between war and wooing, and that natural kinship is called romance. It comes upon a man especially in the great hour of youth; and every man who has ever been young at all has felt, if only for a moment, this ultimate and poetic paradox.

Free Love in Literature[*]

All the most subtle truths of literature are to be found in legend. There is no better test of the truth of serious fiction than the simple truths to be found in a fairy tale or an old ballad. Now, in the whole of folk-lore there is no such thing as free love. There is such a thing as false love. There is also another thing, which the old ballads always talk of as true love. But the story always turns on the keeping of a bond or the breaking of it; and this quite apart from orthodox morality in the matter of the marriage bond. The love may be in the strict sense sinful, but it is never anarchical. There was quite as little freedom for Lancelot as for Arthur; quite as little mere philandering in the philosophy of Tristram as in the philosophy of Galahad. It may have been unlawful love, but it certainly was not lawless love. In the old ballads there is the triumph of true love, as in "The Bailiff's Daughter of Islington"; or the tragedy of true love, as in "Helen of Kirkconnel Lea"; or the tragedy of false love, as in the ballad of "Oh wary, waly up the bank." But there is neither triumph nor tragedy in the idea of *avowedly* transient love; and no literature will ever be made out of it, except the very lightest literature of satire.

* Excerpt was originally published in *Illustrated London News*, July 15, 1922.

And even the satire must be a satire on fickleness, and therefore involve an indirect ideal of fidelity. But you cannot make any enduring literature out of love *conscious* that it will not endure. Even if this mutability were workable as morality, it would still be unworkable as art.

The decadents used to say that things like the marriage vow might be very convenient for commonplace public purposes, but had no place in the world of beauty and imagination. The truth is exactly the other way. The truth is that if marriage had not existed, it would have been necessary for artists to invent it. The truth is that if constancy had never been needed as a social requirement, it would still have been created out of cloud and air as a poetical requirement. If ever monogamy is abandoned in practice, it will linger in legend and in literature. When society is haunted by the butterfly flitting from flower to flower, poetry will still be describing the desire of the moth for the star; and it will be a fixed star. Literature must always revolve round loyalties; for a rudimentary psychological reason, which is simply the nature of narrative. You cannot tell a *story* without the idea of pursuing a purpose and sticking to a point. You cannot tell a story without the idea of the Quest, the idea of the Vow; even if it be only the idea of the Wager.

Perhaps the most modern equivalent to the man who makes a vow is the man who makes a bet. But he must not hedge on a bet; still less must he welsh, or do a bolt when he has made a bet. Even if the story ends with his doing so, the dramatic emotion depends on our realising the dishonesty of his doing so. That is, the drama depends on the keeping or breaking of a bond, if it be only a bet. A man wandering about a race-course, making bets that nobody took seriously, would be merely a bore. And so the hero wandering through a novel, making vows of love that nobody took seriously, is merely a bore. The point here is not so much that morally it cannot be a creditable story, but that artistically it cannot be a story at all. Art is born when the temporary touches the eternal; the shock of beauty is when the irresistible force hits the immovable post.

When once a man looks forward as well as backward to disillusionment, no romance can be made of him. Profligacy may be made romantic, precisely because it implies some betrayal or breaking of a law. But polygamy is not in the least romantic. Polygamy is dull to the point of respectability. When a man looks forward to a number of wives as he does to a number of cigarettes, you can no more make a book out of them than out of the bills from his tobacconist. Anything having the character of a Turkish harem has also something of the character of a Turkey carpet. It is not a portrait, or even a picture, but a pattern. We may at the moment be looking at one highly coloured and even flamboyant figure in the carpet; but we know that on every side, in front as well as behind, the image is repeated without purpose and without finality.

The Next Heresy[*]

The next great heresy is going to be simply an attack on morality; and especially on sexual morality. And it is coming, not from a few Socialists surviving from the Fabian Society, but from the living exultant energy of the rich resolved to enjoy themselves at last, with neither Popery nor Puritanism nor Socialism to hold them back. The thin theory of Collectivism never had any real roots in human nature; but the roots of the new heresy, God knows, are

[*] Excerpt was originally published in *G. K.'s Weekly*, June 19, 1926.

as deep as nature itself, whose flower is the lust of the flesh and the lust of the eye and the pride of life. I say that the man who cannot see this cannot see the signs of the times; cannot see even the sky-signs in the street, that are the new sort of signs in heaven. The madness of to-morrow is not in Moscow, but much more in Manhattan.

A Fury*

All healthy men, ancient and modern, Western and Eastern, hold that there is in sex a fury that we cannot afford to inflame; and that a certain mystery must attach to the instinct if it is to [be] sane. There are people who maintain that they can talk about this topic as coldly and openly as about any other; there are people who maintain that they would walk naked down the street. But these people are not only insane, they are in the most emphatic sense of the word stupid. They do not think; they only point (as children do) and ask "Why?" ... "Why cannot we discuss sex coolly and rationally anywhere?" This is a tired and unintelligent question. It is like asking, "Why does not a man walk on his hands as well as on his feet?" It is silly. If a man walked systematically on his hands, they would not be hands, but feet. And if love or lust were things that we could all discuss without any possible emotion, they would not be love or lust, they would be something else—some mechanical function or abstract natural duty which may or may not exist in animals or in angels, but which has nothing at all to do with sex.... Sex is not an unconscious or innocent thing, but an intense

---

*Excerpt is from "Rabelaisian Regrets", in *The Common Man* (New York: Sheed and Ward, 1950), pp. 125–27.

and powerful thing, a special and violent emotional stimulation that is at once spiritual and physical. A man who asks us to have no emotions in sex is asking us to have no emotions about emotion. . . . It may be said of him, in the strict meaning of the words, that he does not know what he is talking about.

There is such a thing as pornography; as a system of deliberate erotic stimulants. That is not a thing to be argued about with one's intellect, but to be stamped on with one's heel. But the point about it to be noted for our purpose is that this form of excess is separated from the other two by the fact that the motive of it *must* be bad. If a man tries to excite a sex instinct which is too strong already, and that in its meanest form, he *must* be a scoundrel. He is either taking money to degrade his kind or else he is acting on that mystical itch of the evil man to make others evil which is the strangest secret in hell.

Sex and Property[*]

In the dull, dusty, stale, stiff-jointed and lumbering language, to which most modern discussion is limited, it is necessary to say that there is at this moment the same fashionable fallacy about Sex and about Property. In the older and freer language, in which men could both speak and sing, it is truer to say that the same evil spirit has blasted the two great powers that make the poetry of life; the Love of Woman and the Love of the Land. It is important to observe, to start with, that the two things were closely connected so long as humanity was human, even when it was heathen. Nay, they were still closely connected, even

[*] Excerpt is from "Sex and Property", in *The Well and the Shallows*, in *CW*, vol. 3 (San Francisco: Ignatius Press, 1990), pp. 501–3.

when it was a decadent heathenism. But even the stink of decaying heathenism has not been so bad as the stink of decaying Christianity. *Corruptio optimi pessimum* [the corruption of the best].

For instance, there were throughout antiquity, both in its first stage and its last, modes of idolatry and imagery of which Christian men can hardly speak. "Let them not be so much as named among you" [Eph 5:3]. Men wallowed in the mere sexuality of a mythology of sex; they organised prostitution like priesthood, for the service of their temples; they made pornography their only poetry; they paraded emblems that turned even architecture into a sort of cold and colossal exhibitionism. Many learned books have been written of all these phallic cults; and anybody can go to them for the details, for all I care. But what interests me is this:

In one way all this ancient sin was infinitely superior, immeasurably superior, to the modern sin. All those who write of it at least agree on one fact; that it was the cult of Fruitfulness. It was unfortunately too often interwoven, very closely, with the cult of the fruitfulness of the land. It was at least on the side of Nature. It was at least on the side of Life. It has been left to the last Christians, or rather to the first Christians fully committed to blaspheming and denying Christianity, to invent a new kind of worship of Sex, which is not even a worship of Life. It has been left to the very latest Modernists to proclaim an erotic religion which at once exalts lust and forbids fertility. The new Paganism literally merits the reproach of Swinburne, when mourning for the old Paganism: "and rears not the bountiful token and spreads not the fatherly feast." The new priests abolish the fatherhood and keep the feast—to themselves. They are worse than Swinburne's Pagans. The priests of Priapus and Cotytto [fertility deities] go into the kingdom of heaven before them.

Now it is not unnatural that this unnatural separation, between sex and fruitfulness, which even the Pagans would have thought a perversion, has been accompanied with a similar separation and perversion about the nature of the love of the land. In both departments there is precisely the same fallacy; which it is quite possible to state precisely. The reason why our contemporary countrymen do not understand what we mean by Property is that they only think of it in the sense of Money; in the sense of salary; in the sense of something which is immediately consumed, enjoyed and expended; something which gives momentary pleasure and disappears. They do not understand that we mean by Property something that includes that pleasure incidentally; but begins and ends with something far more grand and worthy and creative. The man who makes an orchard where there has been a field, who owns the orchard and decides to whom it shall descend, does also enjoy the taste of apples; and let us hope, also, the taste of cider. But he is doing something very much grander, and ultimately more gratifying, than merely eating an apple. He is imposing his will upon the world in the manner of the charter given him by the will of God; he is asserting that his soul is his own, and does not belong to the Orchard Survey Department, or the chief Trust in the Apple Trade. But he is also doing something which was implicit in all the most ancient religions of the earth; in those great panoramas of pageantry and ritual that followed the order of the seasons in China or Babylonia; he is worshipping the fruitfulness of the world. Now the notion of narrowing property merely to *enjoying* money is exactly like the notion of narrowing love merely to *enjoying* sex. In both cases an incidental, isolated, servile and even secretive pleasure is substituted for participation in a great creative process; even in the everlasting Creation of the world.

3

Marriage ... and Divorce

Creation Day

Between the perfect marriage day
And that fierce future proud, and furled,
I only stole six days—six days
Enough for God to make the world.

For us is a creation made
New moon by night, new sun by day,
That ancient elm that holds the heavens
Sprang to its stature yesterday—

Dearest and first of all things free,
Alone as bride and queen and friend,
Brute facts may come and bitter truths,
But here all doubts shall have an end.

Never again with cloudy talk
Shall life be tricked or faith undone,
The world is many and is made,
But we are sane and we are one.

The essential of [marriage] is that a free man and a free
woman choose to found on earth the only voluntary state;
the only state which creates and loves its own citizens.

— "Marriage and the Modern Mind", *Sidelights*

Marriage is a duel to the death, which no man of honour should decline.

— "The Wild Weddings", *Manalive*

Marriage ... This great human ideal has, like all human ideals, made terrible demands on human nature, and, like all things which men have at any time loved, has surrounded itself with mystery and peril.

— *Speaker*, March 5, 1904

A man once told me that in twenty years I should find married life very difficult. I told him I had found it difficult in twenty minutes; and was indeed aware of it before I began.

— *New Witness*, July 15, 1915

Most husbands are inconvenient; I am one myself.

— *New Witness*, June 3, 1921

I wonder much more at women's patience in time of peace than at their patriotism in time of war. I suspect that the monumental heroism of woman has often been less exhibited, when a man was away for years, than when he was at home for a day. I marvel rather less at the consideration shown him when he has been mangled with a bayonet for the love of his native land; I marvel rather more at the consideration which has prevented his being murdered with a carving knife for his remarks on the Sunday dinner. In short, I am not so much surprised that the great things unite people as I am that the small things do not divide them.

— *New Witness*, May 16, 1919

It is in vain that the modern opponents of marriage tell us that so many marriages are tragic. For the truth is that, however you arrange the rules, or no rules, of the sex relation, however you twist it round or turn it inside out, you cannot make the sex relation anything else but tragic. That is to say, that while the sex relation, or marriage, can be, and I believe generally is, the happiest state for a man, you cannot deprive it of its power to make him the most miserable thing on earth. It is always "for better, for worse." Free love may only be a voluntary bondage. Profligacy may only be a succession of slaveries.

— *Daily News*, October 1, 1904

Marriage is a fact, an actual human relation like that of motherhood, which has certain habits and loyalties, except for a few monstrous cases where it is turned to torture by insanity or sin.

— "The Dramatist", *George Bernard Shaw*

Monogamous marriage proves itself right with every step of existence.

— *Daily News*, October 28, 1905

The notion of regarding divorce as a natural and frequent cure for the normal sorrows of sex came to us chiefly from the millionaire class in America; the coarsest, the most trivial, the most thin-souled, and the most brazenly cruel class that has existed for many centuries.

— *Daily News*, March 12, 1910

The world will always return to monogamy.

— "The Professor Explains",
The Man Who Was Thursday

Two different standards will appear in ordinary morality, and even in ordinary society. Instead of the old social distinction between those who are married and those who

are unmarried, there will be a distinction between those
who are married and those who are really married.

— "The Superstition of Divorce, IV",
The Superstition of Divorce

It is a familiar truth to-day that Progress depends on certain bold experiments, which must often begin by being
lawless that they may become lawful. It is understood in
the subtle compromise of our Constitution (which gives to
each his fitting part) that it is especially the duty of the
Judges to begin this necessary revolution against the law
of the land.... We have had two notable instances of late:
one Judge renouncing the superstition sometimes called
the sanctity of human life, and another Judge eager to
force us to disregard that other superstition called the sanctity of marriage vows.

— *G. K.'s Weekly*, November 12, 1927

The real evil in the change that has been passing over society is the fact that it has sapped foundations; and, worse
still, has not shaken the palaces and spires. It is as if there
were a disease in the world that only devours the bones.
For instance, a Radical fifty years ago would have a generous indignation against the heartless insincerity of the
many State and Society marriages.... Whether or no that
was an abuse to be abolished, we know it has not been
abolished. What has been abolished is the sacrament which
it was supposed to blaspheme. We have not weakened
the gilded parody of marriage; we have only weakened the
marriage. There is not much less of the official loyalty to
a Royal Family; there is only less of the human loyalty
to a family.

— *G. K.'s Weekly*, June 16, 1928

It may be a piece of very silly sentimentalism to represent
the world as full of happy marriages. But to represent the

world as full of happy divorces seems to me much sillier and much more sentimental.

— Illustrated London News, January 25, 1913

Let no one flatter himself that he leaves his family life in search of art, or knowledge; he leaves it because he is fleeing from the baffling knowledge of humanity and from the impossible art of life.

— "A Defence of Bores", *Lunacy and Letters*

When the human tradition of marriage is heavily and seriously disputed, as it is to-day, you can no longer erect any social or moral action upon the basis of it.

— Daily News, October 13, 1906

The wise old fairy tales (which are the wisest things in the world, at any rate the wisest things of worldly origin), the wise old fairy tales never were so silly as to say that the prince and the princess lived peacefully ever afterwards. The fairy tales said that the prince and princess lived happily ever afterwards: and so they did. They lived happily, although it is very likely that from time to time they threw the furniture at each other. Most marriages, I think, are happy marriages; but there is no such thing as a contented marriage. The whole pleasure of marriage is that it is a perpetual crisis.

— "David Copperfield", *Appreciations and Criticisms of the Works of Charles Dickens*

A Defence of Rash Vows[*]

If a prosperous modern man, with a high hat and a frock-coat, were to solemnly pledge himself before all his clerks

[*] "A Defence of Rash Vows", in *The Defendant* (New York: Dodd, Mead & Co., 1904), pp. 18–26.

and friends to count the leaves on every third tree in Holland Walk, to hop up to the City on one leg every Thursday, to repeat the whole of Mill's "Liberty" seventy-six
times, to collect 300 dandelions in fields belonging to anyone of the name of Brown, to remain for thirty-one hours
holding his left ear in his right hand, to sing the names of
all his aunts in order of age on the top of an omnibus, or
make any such unusual undertaking, we should immediately conclude that the man was mad, or, as it is sometimes expressed, was "an artist in life." Yet these vows
are not more extraordinary than the vows which in the
Middle Ages and in similar periods were made, not by
fanatics merely, but by the greatest figures in civic and
national civilization—by kings, judges, poets, and priests.
One man swore to chain two mountains together, and the
great chain hung there, it was said, for ages as a monument
of that mystical folly. Another swore that he would find
his way to Jerusalem with a patch over his eyes, and died
looking for it. It is not easy to see that these two exploits,
judged from a strictly rational standpoint, are any saner
than the acts above suggested. A mountain is commonly a
stationary and reliable object which it is not necessary to
chain up at night like a dog. And it is not easy at first sight
to see that a man pays a very high compliment to the Holy
City by setting out for it under conditions which render it
to the last degree improbable that he will ever get there.
But about this there is one striking thing to be noticed. If
men behaved in that way in our time, we should, as we
have said, regard them as symbols of the "decadence." But
the men who did these things were not decadent; they
belonged generally to the most robust classes of what is
generally regarded as a robust age. Again, it will be urged
that if men essentially sane performed such insanities, it was
under the capricious direction of a superstitious religious

system. This, again, will not hold water; for in the purely terrestrial and even sensual departments of life, such as love and lust, the medieval princes show the same mad promises and performances, the same misshapen imagination and the same monstrous self-sacrifice. Here we have a contradiction, to explain which it is necessary to think of the whole nature of vows from the beginning. And if we consider seriously and correctly the nature of vows, we shall, unless I am much mistaken, come to the conclusion that it is perfectly sane, and even sensible, to swear to chain mountains together, and that, if insanity is involved at all, it is a little insane not to do so.

The man who makes a vow makes an appointment with himself at some distant time or place. The danger of it is that [he] himself should not keep the appointment. And in modern times this terror of one's self, of the weakness and mutability of one's self, has perilously increased, and is the real basis of the objection to vows of any kind. A modern man refrains from swearing to count the leaves on every third tree in Holland Walk, not because it is silly to do so (he does many sillier things), but because he has a profound conviction that before he had got to the three hundred and seventy-ninth leaf on the first tree he would be excessively tired of the subject and want to go home to tea.

In other words, we fear that by that time he will be, in the common but hideously significant phrase, another man. Now, it is this horrible fairy tale of a man constantly changing into other men that is the soul of the decadence. That John Paterson should, with apparent calm, look forward to being a certain General Barker on Monday, Dr. Macgregor on Tuesday, Sir Walter Carstairs on Wednesday, and Sam Slugg on Thursday, may seem a nightmare; but to that nightmare we give the name of modern culture.

One great decadent, who is now dead, published a poem some time ago, in which he powerfully summed up the whole spirit of the movement by declaring that he could stand in the prison yard and entirely comprehend the feelings of a man about to be hanged: "For he that lives more lives than one / More deaths than one must die." And the end of all this is that maddening horror of unreality which descends upon the decadents, and compared with which physical pain itself would have the freshness of a youthful thing. The one hell which imagination must conceive as most hellish is to be eternally acting a play without even the narrowest and dirtiest greenroom in which to be human. And this is the condition of the decadent, of the aesthete, of the free-lover. To be everlastingly passing through dangers which we know cannot scathe us, to be taking oaths which we know cannot bind us, to be defying enemies who we know cannot conquer us—this is the grinning tyranny of decadence which is called freedom.

Let us turn, on the other hand, to the maker of vows. The man who made a vow, however wild, gave a healthy and natural expression to the greatness of a great moment. He vowed, for example, to chain two mountains together, perhaps a symbol of some great relief, or love, or aspiration. Short as the moment of his resolve might be, it was, like all great moments, a moment of immortality, and the desire to say of it *Exegi monumentum aere perennius* ["I have raised a monument more lasting than bronze"] was the only sentiment that would satisfy his mind. The modern aesthetic man would, of course, easily see the emotional opportunity; he would vow to chain two mountains together. But, then, he would quite as cheerfully vow to chain the earth to the moon. And the withering consciousness that he did not mean what he said, that he was, in truth, saying nothing of any great import, would take from him exactly that sense of daring actuality which is the excitement of a vow. For what could be more maddening than an existence in which our mother or aunt received the information that we were going to assassinate the King or build a temple on Ben Nevis with the genial composure of custom?

The revolt against vows has been carried in our day even to the extent of a revolt against the typical vow of marriage. It is most amusing to listen to the opponents of marriage on this subject. They appear to imagine that the ideal of constancy was a yoke mysteriously imposed on mankind by the devil, instead of being, as it is, a yoke consistently imposed by all lovers on themselves. They have invented a phrase, a phrase that is a black and white contradiction in two words—"free-love"—as if a lover ever had been, or ever could be, free. It is the nature of love to bind itself, and the institution of marriage merely paid the average man the compliment of taking him at his word. Modern sages offer to the lover, with an ill-flavoured grin, the largest liberties and the fullest irresponsibility; but they do not respect him as the old Church respected him; they do not write his oath upon the heavens, as the record of his highest moment. They give him every liberty except the liberty to sell his liberty, which is the only one that he wants.

In Mr. Bernard Shaw's brilliant play *The Philanderer*, we have a vivid picture of this state of things. Charteris is a man perpetually endeavouring to be a freelover, which is like endeavouring to be a married bachelor or a white negro. He is wandering in a hungry search for a certain exhilaration which he can only have when he has the courage to cease from wandering. Men knew better than this in old times—in the time, for example, of Shakespeare's heroes. When Shakespeare's men are really celibate they praise the undoubted advantages of celibacy, liberty, irresponsibility, a chance of continual change. But they were not such fools as to continue to talk of liberty when they were in such a condition that they could be made happy or miserable by the moving of someone else's eyebrow. Suckling classes love with debt in his praise of freedom.

> And he that's fairly out of both
> Of all the world is blest.
> He lives as in the golden age,
> When all things made were common;
> He takes his pipe, he tales his glass,
> He fears no man or woman.

This is a perfectly possible, rational and manly position. But what have lovers to do with ridiculous affectations of fearing no man or woman? They know that in the turning of a hand the whole cosmic engine to the remotest star may become an instrument of music or an instrument of torture. They hear a song older than Suckling's, that has survived a hundred philosophies. "Who is this that looketh out of the window, fair as the sun, clear as the moon, terrible as an army with banners?" [Song 6:10].

As we have said, it is exactly this backdoor, this sense of having a retreat behind us, that is, to our minds, the sterilizing spirit in modern pleasure. Everywhere there is the persistent and insane attempt to obtain pleasure without paying for it. Thus, in politics the modern Jingoes practically say, "Let us have the pleasures of conquerors without the pains of soldiers: let us sit on sofas and be a hardy race." Thus, in religion and morals, the decadent mystics say: "Let us have the fragrance of sacred purity without the sorrows of self-restraint; let us sing hymns alternately to the Virgin and Priapus." Thus in love the free-lovers say: "Let us have the splendour of offering ourselves without the peril of committing ourselves; let us see whether one cannot commit suicide an unlimited number of times." Emphatically it will not work. There are thrilling moments, doubtless, for the spectator, the amateur, and the aesthete; but there is one thrill that is known only to the soldier who fights for his own flag, to the ascetic who starves himself for his own illumination, to the lover who makes finally his own choice. And it is this transfiguring self-discipline that makes the vow a truly sane thing. It must have satisfied even the giant hunger of the soul of a lover or a poet to know that in consequence of some one instant of decision that strange chain would hang for centuries in the Alps among the silences of stars and snows. All around us is the city of small sins, abounding in backways and retreats, but surely, sooner or later, the towering flame will rise from the harbour announcing that the reign of the cowards is over and a man is burning his ships.

The Decay of Honour[*]

There is one point which Catholics or Moslems or men of any other continuous or dignified traditions will mention immediately about marriage; and it is the one thing that is now never mentioned at all. It is what used to be called "keeping your word," and the world seems to have forgotten all about it.

In short, our journalists do not realise that the human race has any respect for coherency of mind. It is not strange that their world has also lost all respect for that other sort of coherency which was called integrity. Especially that simplest form of it, which says that a man should not break

[*] Excerpt was originally published in *G. K.'s Weekly*, January 23, 1932.

a promise; that a man should not make a promise, if he thinks he is certain to break it. It is, as a stark staring fact, the very backbone of the question of the marriage vow; but nobody even mentions it when discussing marriage. One journalist pours out a torrent of sob-stuff over the "innocent" parties who have been married in a church, and want to be remarried in a church after a divorce; and he never even mentions it. He says over and over again, with monotonous fury, that they have committed no offence. Now we all, I hope, feel compassion and sympathy for people in such tragic entanglements, whether we think, on general grounds, that they should be loosened from their vows or not. But to say they commit no offence is infernal nonsense. They commit an offence which, if they committed it in a law-court instead of a church, would land them in jail. They have sworn, exactly as men swear in a law-court, calling on God as a witness, that they will keep themselves only for each other till death do them part. The language is as plain and definite as anything legal or criminal could possibly be. To falsify such an oath is perjury; and we can all imagine a score of cases in which perjury would be a huge human temptation, or even a very excusable misdeed. But these people are actually offended because, while their perjury is officially condoned and permitted, they are not allowed to go back and take another and contrary vow, breaking their first, in the very same place where they made their first. There is not a law-court in the world that would allow itself to be insulted like that.

In the bottomless confusion and botheration wherein they dwell, the Divorce Party will very probably answer that such vows of fidelity till death are too stringent, and should be softened. Which is (as any chance person still visited by a ray of reason will perceive) a very good reason for not being married in a church. That is why they would use it as a reason for insisting on being married in a church. I doubt if there has ever been, since humanity was above brutes, such brutal and bewildering stupidity as the position of the person who is commended to us in these appeals: a person who disapproves of the Church vows, therefore insists on taking them, then insists on breaking them, then insists on receiving the same blessing for breaking them as for taking them; and finally takes them all over again, with the utmost solemnity, after discovering how easy they are to break. But what concerns us, from the secular standpoint of our social policy, is this vast and ghastly gap in the sense of personal responsibility and reliability. Men mention thousands of other things; but they do not even mention this question of the keeping or breaking of a promise. They consider the matter of marriage in relation to happiness, to convention, to liberty, to legality; but never once, not even by chance, do they think of it, or think that anybody could think of it, in relation to honour. Now this is a very serious state of the public mind, or mindlessness; especially for us, who would seek to rebuild society upon a myriad of experiments in personal responsibility and manhood. Whatever else a society has, it cannot have this chaotic view of contracts and engagements; and it looks as if we should have to break through the ring of the press monopoly before we can begin to teach a more loyal and consistent view of life.

Marriage and the Modern Mind[*]

I have been requested to write something about Marriage and the Modern Mind. It would perhaps be more appropriate to write about Marriage and the Modern Absence

---

[*] "Marriage and the Modern Mind", in *Sidelights on New London and Newer York*, in *CW*, vol. 21 (San Francisco: Ignatius Press, 1990), pp. 515–20.

of Mind. In much of their current conduct, those who call themselves "Modern" seem to have abandoned the use of reason; they have sunk back into their own subconsciousness, perhaps under the influence of the psychology now most fashionable in the drawing-room; and it is an understatement to say that they act more automatically than the animals. Wives and husbands seem to leave home more in the manner of somnambulists.

If anybody thinks I exaggerate the mindlessness of modern comment on this matter, I am content to refer him to the inscription under a large photograph of a languishing lady, in the newspaper now before me. It states that the lady has covered herself with glory as the inventor of "Companionate Divorce." It goes on to state, in her own words, that she will marry her husband again if he asks her again; and that she has been living with him ever since she was divorced from him. If mortal muddle-headedness can go deeper than that, in this vale of tears, I should like to see it. The newspaper picture and paragraph I can actually see; and stupidity so stupendous as that has never been known in human history before. The first thing to say about marriage and the modern mind, therefore, is that it is natural enough that people with no mind should want to have no marriage.

But there is another simple yet curious illustration of modern stupidity in the matter. And that is that, while I have known thousands of people arguing about marriage, sometimes furiously against it, sometimes rather feebly in favour of it, I have never known any one of the disputants begin by asking what marriage is. They nibble at it with negative criticism; they chip pieces off it and exhibit them as specimens, called "hard cases"; they treat every example of the rule as an exception to the rule; but they never look at the rule. They never ask, even in the name of history or human curiosity, what the thing is, or why it is, or why the overwhelming mass of mankind believes that it must be. Let us begin with the alphabet, as one does with infants.

Marriage, humanly considered, rests upon a fact of human nature, which we may call a fact of natural history. All the higher animals require much longer parental protection than do the lower; the baby elephant is a baby much longer than the baby jellyfish. But even beyond this natural tutelage, man needs something quite unique in nature. Man alone needs education. I know that animals train their young in particular tricks; as cats teach kittens to catch mice. But this is a very limited and rudimentary education. It is what the hustling millionaires call Business Education; that is not education at all. Even at that, I doubt whether any pupil presenting himself for Matriculation or entrance into Standard VI, would now be accepted if flaunting the stubborn boast of a capacity to catch mice. Education is a complex and many-sided culture to meet a complex and many-sided world; and the animals, especially the lower animals, do not require it. It is said that the herring lays thousands of eggs in a day. But, though evidently untouched by the stunt of Birth-Control, in other ways the herring is highly modern. The mother herring has no need to remember her own children, and certainly therefore, no need to remember her own mate. But then the duties of a young herring, just entering upon life, are very simple and largely instinctive; they come, like a modern religion, from within. A herring does not have to be taught to take a bath; for he never takes anything else. He does not have to be trained to take off a hat to a lady herring, for he never puts on a hat, or any other Puritanical disguise to hamper the Greek grace of his movements. Consequently his father and mother have no common task or responsibility; and they can safely model their union upon the boldest and most advanced of the new novels and plays. Doubtless the female herring does say to the male herring, "True marriage must be free from the dogmas of priests; it must be a thing of one exquisite moment." Doubtless the male herring does say to the female herring, "When Love has died in the heart, Marriage is a mockery in the home."

This philosophy, common among the lower forms of life, is obviously of no use among the higher. This way of talking, however suitable for herrings, or even for rats and rabbits, who are said to be so prolific, does not meet the case of the creature endowed with reason. The young of the human species, if they are to reach the full possibilities of the human culture, so various, so laborious, so elaborate, must be under the protection of responsible persons through very long periods of mental and moral growth. I know there are some who grow merely impatient and irrational at this point; and say they could do just as well without education. But they lie; for they could not even express that opinion, if they had not laboriously learnt one particular language in which to talk nonsense. The moment we have realized this, we understand why the relations of the sexes normally remain static; and in most cases, permanent. For though, taking this argument alone, there would be a case for the father and mother parting when the children were mature, the number of people who at the age of fifty really wish to bolt with the typist or be abducted by the chauffeur is less than is now frequently supposed.

Well, even if the family held together as long as that, it would be better than nothing; but in fact even such belated divorce is based on bad psychology. All the modern licence is based on bad psychology; because it is based on the latest psychology. And that is like knowing the last proposition in Euclid without knowing the first. It is the first elements of psychology that the people called "modern" do not know. One of the things they cannot comprehend is the thing called "atmosphere"; as they show by shrieking with derision when anybody demands "a religious atmosphere" in the schools. The atmosphere of something safe and settled can only exist where people see it in the future as well as in the past. Children know exactly what is meant by having really come home; and the happier of them keep something of the feeling as they grow up. But they cannot keep the feeling for ten minutes, if there is an assumption that Papa is only waiting for Tommy's twenty-first birthday to carry the typist off to Trouville; or that the chauffeur actually has the car at the door, that Mrs. Brown may go off the moment Miss Brown has "come out."

That is, in practical experience, the basic idea of marriage; that the founding of a family must be on a firm foundation; that the rearing of the immature must be protected by something patient and enduring. It is the common conclusion of all mankind; and all common sense is on its side. A small minority of what may be called the idle Intelligentsia, have, just recently and in our corner of the world, criticized this idea of Marriage in the name of what they call the Modern Mind. The first obvious or apparent question is how they deal with the practical problem of children. The first apparent answer is that they do not deal with it at all.

At best, they propose to get rid of babies, or the problem of babies, in one of three typically modern ways. One is to say that there shall be no babies. This suggestion may be addressed to the individual; but it is addressed to every individual. Another is that the father should instantly send the babies, especially if they are boys, to a distant and inaccessible school, with bounds like a prison, that the babies may become men, in a manner that is considered impossible in the society of their own father. But this is rapidly ceasing to be a Modern method; and even the Moderns have found that it is rather behind the times. The third way, which is unimpeachably Modern, is to imitate Rousseau, who left his baby on the door-step of the Foundling Hospital. It is true that, among the Moderns, it is generally nothing so human or traditional as the Foundling Hospital. The baby is to be left on the doorstep of the State Department for Education and Universal Social Adjustment. In short, these people mean, with various degrees of vagueness, that the place of the Family can now be taken by the State.

The difficulty of the first method, and so far, of the second and third, is that they may be carried out. The suggestion is made to everybody in the hope that it will not be accepted by everybody; it is offered to all in the hope that it may not be accepted by all. If *nobody* has any children, everybody can still be satisfied by Birth-Control methods and justified by Birth-Control arguments. Even the reformers do not want this; but they cannot offer any objection to any individual—or every individual. In somewhat the same way, Rousseau may act as an individual and not as a social philosopher, but he could not prevent all the other individuals acting as individuals. And if all the babies born in the world were left on the door-step of the Foundling Hospital, the Hospital, and the door-step, would have to be considerably enlarged. Now something like this is what has really happened, in the vague and drifting centralization of our time. The hospital has been enlarged into the School and then into the State; not the guardian of some abnormal children, but the guardian of all normal children. Modern mothers and fathers, of the emancipated sort, could not do their quick-change acts of bewildering divorce and scattered polygamy, if they did not believe in a big benevolent Grandmother, who could ultimately take over ten million children by very grandmotherly legislation.

This modern notion about the State is a delusion. It is not founded on the history of real States, but entirely on reading about unreal or ideal States, like the Utopias of Mr. Wells. The real State, though a necessary human combination, always has been and always will be, far too large, loose, clumsy, indirect and even insecure, to be the "home" of the human young who are to be trained in the human tradition. If mankind had not been organized into families, it would never have had the organic power to be organized into commonwealths. Human culture is handed down in the customs of countless households; it is the only way in which human culture can remain human. The households are right to confess a common loyalty or federation under some king or republic. But the king cannot be the nurse in every nursery; or even the government become the governess in every schoolroom. Look at the real story of States, modern as well as ancient, and you will see a dissolving view of distant and uncontrollable things, making up most of the politics of the earth. Take the most populous centre. China is now called a Republic. In consequence it is ruled by five contending armies and is much less settled than when it was an Empire. What has preserved China has been its domestic religion. South America, like all Latin lands, is full of domestic graces and gaieties; but it is governed by a series of revolutions. We ourselves may be governed by a Dictator; or by a General Strike; or by a banker living in New York. Government grows more elusive every day. But the traditions of humanity support humanity; and the central one is this tradition of Marriage.

And the essential of it is that a free man and a free woman choose to found on earth the only voluntary state; the only state which creates and which loves its citizens. So long as these real responsible beings stand together, they can survive all the vast changes, deadlocks and disappointments, which make up mere political history. But if they fail each other, it is as certain as death that "the State" will fail them.

Incompatible[*]

In everything on this earth that is worth doing, there is a stage when no one would do it, except for necessity or honor. It is then that the Institution upholds a man and helps him on to the firmer ground ahead. Whether this solid fact of human nature is sufficient to justify the sublime dedication of Christian marriage is quite another matter, it is amply sufficient to justify the general human feeling of marriage as a fixed thing, dissolution of which is a fault or, at least, an ignominy. The essential element is not so much duration as security. Two people must be tied together in order to do themselves justice; for twenty minutes at a dance, or for twenty years in a marriage. In both cases the point is, that if a man is bored in the first five minutes he must go on and force himself to be happy. Coercion is a kind of encouragement; and anarchy (or what some call liberty) is essentially oppressive, because it is essentially discouraging. If we all floated in the air like bubbles, free to drift anywhere at any instant, the practical result would be that no one would have the courage to begin a conversation. It would be so embarrassing to

[*]Excerpt is from "The Free Family", *What's Wrong with the World*, in *CW* 4:197.

start a sentence in a friendly whisper, and then have to shout the last half of it because the other party was floating away into the free and formless ether. The two must hold each other to do justice to each other. If Americans can be divorced for "incompatibility of temper" I cannot conceive why they are not all divorced. I have known many happy marriages, but never a compatible one. The whole aim of marriage is to fight through and survive the instant when incompatibility becomes unquestionable. For a man and a woman, as such, are incompatible.

The Freedom of Marriage[*]

Marriage is a bond because it has not arisen in bondage. It is one of the very few things still remaining that are, in their origin, free. I must not personally make war, for that is called assault and battery; when it is not called being drunk and disorderly. I must not make mischief; for that, even when it is justified, is called libel and slander. I must not make a demonstration; for that is more and more being treated like making a nuisance. One form of mystical manufacture remains to the individual citizen, and has not been taken over by the materialistic manufacturers: he is still allowed to make love.

Now, it is wholly and solely because the thing arises in this independent atmosphere that it has ever claimed this eternal validity. In other words, marriage is not a matter of contract. It is not even a matter of honesty. It is a matter of honour. And those benighted beings who imagine that honesty is the same as honour may be easily excused for having the delusion that divorce is much the

[*] Excerpt was originally published in *Daily News*, December 7, 1912.

same as marriage. Honesty means giving two halfpennies
in exchange for one penny; and if this quaint custom were
adopted, it would probably revolutionise the world, and
certainly improve it.

But honour means something quite different from giving two halfpennies for a penny. Honour means never
giving a blank cheque till you really mean to give it; and
then never going back from it, though it were filled up
for millions. The two essentials of an act involving honour
are agnosticism and tenacity. Or (if you prefer to put it so)
ignorance and obstinacy. Or, again (if you are the slave of
superstition), faith, and fidelity. I am not concerned with
words, but with meanings: and all those three phrases mean
the same thing. But I think no phrase can improve on that
oath which most men have taken and nearly all men have
heard—"For better for worse, for richer for poorer, in
sickness and in health." No man who understood the idea
of honour has ever heard those words unmoved.

But my purpose here is only to insist that the final fixity
of marriage could have no origin except in the freedom of
marriage. It is the most irrevocable of all modern acts, because it is the most voluntary of all modern acts. That practical instinct which is present wherever religion is present
makes the priest warn the bride and bridegroom, even at
the altar, against doing what they are doing. Whether the
registrar offers a similar warning I shall never know; for
my conscience and inclination forbid me to have a new
wife, and my commonsense forbids me to expect a wife to
get married again. My concern here is simply that the
thing called loyalty cannot exist unless it springs out of
the thing called liberty. Those who say that marriage is a
lottery have, for a moment, a glimmer of sense in their
senseless heads. For a lottery has only one virtue; you can
keep out of it if you like. All that people call the rigidity of

marriage reposes on the fact that people can keep out of it if they like. But if once that high and civilized liberty were taken away, the whole idea of civilized loyalty would be taken away with it. If my old friends the Eugenists had, violently and by pure police force, mated me with a woman—I should not feel the faintest moral obligation to be faithful to her. It may or may not be immoral to make a bet. It is most unquestionably immoral to make a bet compulsory.

This is where both the Reports recently issued about divorce may probably do harm from the beginning. They both obscurely suggest that a man is a free man when he is divorced. The truth is that he is never so free a man as at the moment when he is married. It is only a pack of more or less tyrannical lawyers who decide that he shall be divorced; it is he who decides that he will be married. That this liberty involves a loyalty, and that loyalty may involve a tragedy—all that is logically involved in the very nature of loyalty and liberty. A man cannot be free unless he is free to promise; a man cannot promise unless he is ready to keep his promise. If there is a grievance in this, it is the grievance felt by black because it is not white, or by the word "Yes" because it cannot attain the splendid nihilism of being the word "No." And divorce is not an emancipation. It is a veto: because it is a veto on the most human of things—vows.

An imprudent marriage is one of the few entirely free things which a poor man is still free to do. And the freedom is not anarchic; the freedom is heroic; precisely because its consequences are fixed. All our legislation for some time past and (I greatly fear) for some time to come, is a legislation which, for good or evil, leaves the poor less liberty; that is, less responsibility and choice. And this new claim of upper class magistrates or upper middle-class juries to violate people's vows for them will be precisely as aristocratic an interference with sex as any of the alleged *droits de seigneur* ["the rights of the lord", i.e., the supposed privilege of a feudal lord to sleep with the bride of any of his vassals]. If marriage is attacked to-day, it will not be because it is a lingering tyranny, but because it is the last of the free institutions.

The Bonds of Love[*]

The New Woman's monologue wearies, not because it is unwomanly, but because it is inhuman. It exhibits the most exhausting of combinations: the union of fanaticism of speech with frigidity of soul—the things that made Robespierre seem a monster. The worst example I remember was one trumpeted in a Review: a lady doctor, who has ever afterwards haunted me as a sort of nightmare of spiritual imbecility. I forget her exact words, but they were to the effect that sex and motherhood should be treated neither with ribaldry nor reverence: "It is too serious a subject for ribaldry, and I myself cannot understand reverence towards anything that is physical." There, in a few words, is the whole twisted and tortured priggishness which poisons the present age. The person who cannot laugh at sex ought to be kicked; and the person who cannot reverence pain ought to be killed. Until that lady doctor gets a little ribaldry and a little reverence into her soul, she has no right to have any opinion at all about the affairs of humanity.

Miss Florence Farr, the author of *Modern Woman*, is bitten a little by the mad dog of modernity, the habit of dwelling

[*] Excerpt was originally published in *Illustrated London News*, June 25 and July 2, 1910.

disproportionally on the abnormal and the diseased; but she writes rationally and humorously, like a human being; she sees that there are two sides to the case; and she even puts in a fruitful suggestion that, with its subconsciousness and its virtues of the vegetable, the new psychology may turn up on the side of the old womanhood. One may say indeed that in such a book as this our amateur philosophising of today is seen at its fairest; and even at its fairest it exhibits certain qualities of bewilderment and disproportion which are somewhat curious to note.

I think the oddest thing about the advanced people is that, while they are always talking of things as problems, they have hardly any notion of what a real problem is. A real problem only occurs when there are admittedly disadvantages in all courses that can be pursued . . . or because there are in it incompatible advantages. Now if woman is simply the domestic slave that many of these writers represent, if man has bound her by brute force, if he has simply knocked her down and sat on her—then there is no problem about the matter. She has been locked in the kitchen and ought to be let out. If there is any problem of sex, it must be because the case is not so simple as that; because there is something to be said for the man as well as for the woman; and because there are evils in unlocking the kitchen door, in addition to the obvious good of it.

Now, I will take two instances from Miss Farr's own book of problems that are really problems, and which she entirely misses because she will not admit that they are problematical.

The writer asks the substantial question squarely enough: "Is indissoluble marriage good for mankind?" and she answers it squarely enough: "For the great mass of mankind, yes." To those like myself, who move in the old-world dream of Democracy, that admission ends the whole question. There may be exceptional people who would be happier without Civil Government; sensitive souls who really feel unwell when they see a policeman. But we have surely the right to impose the State on everybody if it suits nearly everybody; and if so, we have the right to impose the Family on everybody if it suits nearly everybody. But the queer and cogent point is this: that Miss Farr does not see the real difficulty about allowing exceptions—the real difficulty that has made most legislators reluctant to allow them. I do not say there should be no exceptions, but I do say that the author has not seen the painful problem of permitting any.

The difficulty is simply this: that if it comes to claiming exceptional treatment, the very people who will claim it will be those who least deserve it. The people who are quite convinced they are superior are the very inferior people; the men who really think themselves extraordinary are the most ordinary rotters on earth. If you say that marriage is for common people, but divorce for free and noble spirits, all the weak and selfish people will dash for the divorce; while the few free and noble spirits you wish to help will very probably (because they are free and noble) go on wrestling with the marriage. For it is one of the marks of real dignity of character not to wish to separate oneself from the honour and tragedy of the whole tribe. All men are ordinary men; the extraordinary men are those who know it.

As I was saying, our makers of ultramodern moralities (and immoralities) do not really grasp how problematical a problem is. They are not specially the people who see the difficulties of modern life; rather, they are the people who do not see the difficulties. These innovators make life insanely simple; making freedom or knowledge a universal pill. Miss Florence Farr's proposition that marriage is good for the common herd, but can be advantageously violated by special "experimenters" and pioneers, takes no account of the problem of the disease of pride. It is easy enough to say that weaker souls had better be guarded, but that we must give freedom to Georges Sand or make exceptions for George Eliot. The practical puzzle is this: that it is precisely the weakest sort of lady novelist who thinks she is Georges Sand; it is precisely the silliest woman who is sure she is George Eliot. It is the small soul that is sure it is an exception; the large soul is only too proud to be the rule. To advertise for exceptional people is to collect all the sulks and sick fancies and futile ambitions of the earth. The good artist is he who can be understood; it is the bad artist who is always "misunderstood."

But in Miss Farr's entertaining pages there is another instance of the same thing. She disposes of the difficult question of vows and bonds in love by leaving out altogether the one extraordinary fact of experience on which the whole matter turns. She again solves the problem by assuming that it is not a problem. Concerning oaths of fidelity, etc., she writes: "We cannot trust ourselves to make a real love-knot unless money or custom forces us to 'bear and forbear.' There is always the lurking fear that we shall not be able to keep faith unless we swear upon the Book. This is, of course, not true of young lovers. Every first love is born free of tradition; indeed, not only is first love innocent and valiant, but it sweeps aside all the wise laws it has been taught, and burns away experience in its own light. The revelation is so extraordinary, so unlike anything told by the poets, so absorbing, that it is impossible to believe that the feeling can die out."

Now this is exactly as if some old naturalist settled the bat's place in nature by saying boldly, "Bats do not fly." It is as if he solved the problem of whales by bluntly declaring

that whales live on land. There is a problem of vows, as of
bats and whales. What Miss Farr says about it is quite lucid
and explanatory; it simply happens to be flatly untrue. It
is not the fact that young lovers have no desire to swear
on the Book. They are always at it. It is not the fact that
every young love is born free of traditions about binding
and promising, about bonds and signatures and seals. On
the contrary, lovers wallow in the wildest pedantry and
precision about these matters. They do the craziest things
to make their love legal and irrevocable. They tattoo each
other with promises; they cut into rocks and oaks with their
names and vows; they bury ridiculous things in ridiculous
places to be a witness against them; they bind each other
with rings, and inscribe each other in Bibles; if they are raving lunatics (which is not untenable), they are mad solely
on this idea of binding and on nothing else. It is quite true
that the tradition of their fathers and mothers is in favour
of fidelity; but it is emphatically not true that the lovers
merely follow it; they invent it anew. It is quite true that the
lovers feel their love eternal, and independent of oaths; but
it is emphatically not true that they do not desire to take the
oaths. They have a ravening thirst to take as many oaths as
possible. Now this is the paradox; this is the whole problem.
It is not true, as Miss Farr would have it, that young people feel free of vows, being confident of constancy; while
old people invent vows, having lost that confidence. That
would be much too simple; if that were so there would be
no problem at all. The startling but quite solid fact is that
young people are especially fierce in making fetters and final
ties at the very moment when they think them unnecessary.
The time when they want the vow is exactly the time when
they do not need it. That is worth thinking about.

Nearly all the fundamental facts of mankind are to be
found in its fables. And there is a singularly sane truth in

all the old stories of the monsters—such as centaurs, mermaids, sphinxes, and the rest. It will be noted that in each of these the humanity, though imperfect in its extent, is perfect in its quality. The mermaid is half a lady and half a fish; but there is nothing fishy about the lady. A centaur is half a gentleman and half a horse. But there is nothing horsey about the gentleman. The centaur is a manly sort of man—up to a certain point. The mermaid is a womanly woman—so far as she goes. The human parts of the monsters are handsome, like heroes, or lovely, like nymphs; their bestial appendages do not affect the full perfection of their humanity—what there is of it. There is nothing humanly wrong with the centaur, except that he rides a horse without a head. There is nothing humanly wrong with the mermaid; Hood put a good comic motto to his picture of a mermaid: "All's well that ends well." It is, perhaps, quite true; it all depends which end. Those old wild images included a crucial truth. Man is a monster. And he is all the more a monster because one part of him is perfect. It is not true, as the evolutionists say, that man moves perpetually up a slope from imperfection to perfection, changing ceaselessly, so as to be suitable. The immortal part of a man and the deadly part are jarringly distinct and have always been. And the best proof of this is in such a case as we have considered—the case of the oaths of love.

A man's soul is as full of voices as a forest; there are ten thousand tongues there like all the tongues of the trees: fancies, follies, memories, madnesses, mysterious fears, and more mysterious hopes. All the settlement and sane government of life consists in coming to the conclusion that some of those voices have authority and others not. You may have an impulse to fight your enemy or an impulse to run away from him; a reason to serve your country or a reason to betray it; a good idea for making sweets or a better idea for poisoning them. The only test I know by which to judge one argument or inspiration from another is ultimately this: that all the noble necessities of man talk the language of eternity. When man is doing the three or four things that he was sent on this earth to do, then he speaks like one who shall live for ever. A man dying for his country does not talk as if local preferences could change. When men are making commonwealths, they talk in terms of the absolute, and so they do when they are making (however unconsciously) those smaller commonwealths which are called families. There are in life certain immortal moments, moments that have authority. Lovers are right to tattoo each other's skins and cut each other's names about the world; they do belong to each other in a more awful sense than they know.

Scientific Marriage*

I have received one or two letters on ... my allusion to "the maniacs" who proposed scientifically to superintend marriage and a choice of mates. This is rendered all the more interesting because there has been a suggestive correspondence of late in *The Morning Leader* upon much the same matter. In that correspondence the chief thing that I remember was the fact that a lady wrote urging what appears to me the very obvious and wholesome point of view of the need of freedom and chivalry in sexual choice and was informed for her pains that she wrote like a romantic girl, which seemed to me to be a very complimentary description. A romantic girl means simply in another and inferior language a normal female person at the most active

*Excerpt was originally published in *Daily News*, January 28, 1905.

and important age. In fact, there is nothing else very much worth being but a romantic girl, unless you have the good fortune to be a romantic boy. But since so many of my correspondents seemed really to think that I was using a strong expression in calling the supporters of the expert authority in marriage by the name of "maniacs," I will take this opportunity very briefly of repeating the offensive epithet, and of adding a very rough and general explanation. Suffice it to say, by way of general statement of my position, that I think that in this matter, as in many others, modern science is acting as a thoroughly morbid influence. It is seeking to remove disease by treating everyone as an invalid.

There are, no doubt, innumerable objections of detail, innumerable practical objections to this proposal of hygienic humanity; but practical objections can generally be got over. The final objection to a scheme is that it is undesirable; there is always some hope for it, such is the ardent chivalry of man, so long as it is merely impossible. It is not because we could not make marriages scientific that we resent the conception; it is because we do not want to make them scientific. Conservative philosophers have always followed a very mistaken course in endeavoring to avert social reconstructions or developments by denouncing them as what they call outside the sphere of practical politics. For the soul of man is itself outside the sphere of practical politics, and the one thing that really cannot be changed is our love of the difficult and unattainable. Humanity is always young, and it is an imprudent course with young people to dissuade them from an action by daring them to do it.

But the real objection of the scientific marriage is that it is part of a large modern mistake. Whence came this extraordinary idea that being healthy has something to do with being careful? Clearly the reverse is true. It is being careless that has to do with being healthy. The condition of carelessness is the condition of joy, it is the condition of strength and normality. In particular and abnormal individual cases we have to impose care, but even then the care is a sign and blazon of plague and sickness, like the cross on the old doors of London. But when we are dealing with humanity, as we are in all such proposals of a sociological and political character, it is surely obvious that care is the very last thing we should recommend. For care is, as I say, personal and abnormal; hygiene is itself a disease. A man may be forced to be cautious; but humanity should be recklessness itself. For the high and natural thing is to do everything that is healthy, not for the sake of health but for the sake of joy.

The man who walks to Brighton for the sake of his health will perhaps do himself some good. But the man who walks to Brighton for the sake of Brighton (if such a man exists) will do himself much more. The man who exercises with Indian clubs in order to train his muscles may to some extent train them. But the man who exercises with a cricket bat in order to pull down the arrogance of Hampshire will exercise them much more.

Health will only visit those who do not think of her, but of her rivals. Her rivals may be anything, climbing roofs, collecting beetles, serenading a lady.

And that which is true of all other forms of human satisfaction is true also of the question of marriage. The man who best advances health by walking is the man who wishes to get to the top of a particular hill. The man who most advances health by playing tennis or golf or football is the man who wishes at a particular moment to win a particular match. And the man who most advances health in his conduct relating to marriage is the man who wishes, to the exclusion of everything else, to marry a particular

woman. It may happen, of course, that the marriage ends
in a calamity by one of the parties killing the other, or
transmitting some hereditary curse. But so equally it may
happen that the ardour of the pedestrian wishing to climb
a particular hill may end in calamity, in his falling over
an abrupt precipice on the other side. But the latter inci-
dent does not alter the fact that an ardour to reach heights
and view great scenery is the right spirit for most men to
undertake a walk, nor does the former tragedy alter the
fact that the right spirit for men as a whole to undertake
marriage relations is a spirit of free selection and powerful personal attachment. And, indeed, we must of necessity go somewhat further than this. A wise student of real
human hygiene would encourage his followers to engage
in the main in healthy exercises, even if they were dangerous, and he would very rapidly find, I think, that the
most healthy of them were the most dangerous of all. He
would permit his mountaineering followers to rush up hill
even if he knew that a certain considerable minority of
hills had precipices on the other side of them. And just
as a disregard of the danger of cliffs is part not merely of
the joy of the mountaineer, but actually of the health
of the mountaineer, so an indifference to the dangers of
science and heredity is a part not merely of the joy of the
lover, but actually of the health of the lover.

On Divorce and Divinity[*]

It may or may not be true that the same authority which
says that marriages are made in heaven, says that some are
not made in heaven, and therefore simplifies their problems

[*] Excerpt was originally published in *New Witness*, May 24, 1918.

on earth. It may be that the very existence and acceptance of this supernormal thing does combine sympathy for the exception with sanctity for the rule; as it combines, for the saint, the fact of being superior with the sense of being inferior. I do not deny that it can do it; for it is a point on which I have no claim to speak. What I do deny is that Mr. Haynes and his rapid reform can do it. What I do deny is that "hustling" legal gentlemen and payments "in cash" can do it. Whether or no marriage is maintained when a man can be absolved by a power he regards as divine, I say it is not maintained if he can practically absolve himself, by disappearing for three years. Whether or no it be enough that a supernormal power denies a supernormal debt, I say it is not enough that a man pays for his fun by flinging a handful of money at his wife, as he might easily have to do with his mistress. This does not approach the solid social object I need; the general assumption that a man of honour does not finally desert his family, as a patriot does not finally desert his country. Least of all do I admit that the sort of men who make our laws can be trusted to unmake our marriages.

Murder and Marriage[*]

For a long time, and indeed up to the present time, it has been my joy to boast that Crime Stories are the only really moral tales in modern fiction. The quiet tales of the home and the family, the talk over the tea-cups, the cosy idyll of the fireside, all that was becoming more and more wild with profligacy and polygamy—crawling with divorced

[*] Excerpt was originally published in *G. K.'s Weekly*, April 5, 1934.

wives and disguised mistresses; so that it was only necessary to read the first page or two, about the neat cushions
and home-made cakes of the universally respected Lee-
Lumpkins, or the peace of the Hugby home in its dear old
home-town, in order to be quite certain that three-quarters
of the characters were bigamists or brides who bolted to
Reno with the chauffeur. But while the demure domestic novel of cakes and curtains became deliriously immoral,
the dark detective tale of blood and bludgeons, of poison
and poignards, of cutting throats and crushing skulls with
some heavy blunt instrument—that remained as pure as the
Maiden's Prayer and as moral as Sandford and Merton. The
prim and proper old lady, the shy and bashful young person
(if any such remain), had to take refuge in reading "The
Gory Golf-Club," or "The Corpse in the Clothes-Basket,"
simply because there was nothing else sufficiently quiet and
harmless to read. We despised scribblers of murder stories
alone upheld the ancient standards of Purity and Peace in
the Home. That home might be slightly ruffled, from time
to time, by the wife finding the husband with his brains
untidily distributed over the breakfast table, or the husband
finding the wife hanging head downwards in the well. But
normally there was a certain presumption that she was a
wife or that he was a husband; or at least that they lost something of their Lee-Lumpkins status if they were not. There
might be a temporary mystery about which was the villain
and which the virtuous person, but there was no mystery
at all about what was villainy and what was virtue. People
were doubtful about whether they had got the wrong murderer, but they were not doubtful about whether murder
was wrong; as most people in most ordinary modern novels are obviously doubtful about whether marriage is right.
It is only just very lately that I have begun to observe a

difference. And the difference interests me enormously; for I profoundly disbelieve in all the sophistry that is used to attack marriage, and I am horribly amused to see it beginning to be used in order to defend murder. If I had a supernatural and miraculous gift of prophecy, like Mr. H. G. Wells, I should be inclined to predict that fifty years hence the police novel will have become a new kind of problem novel, which will justify a wife destroying her husband, exactly as the present problem novels justify her divorcing her husband. I have read recently about six detective stories, and these among the most intelligent and the best written, which really justify the murder, or the private killing of a man, on the ground that a man can be such a nuisance that there is nothing to be done but to kill him. All the excellent arguments for divorce are also excellent arguments for death. It constantly happens that divorce would not be so effective as death; that the obnoxious person has for other reasons some power of revenge, financial or psychological, which makes him troublesome as long as he is alive. In that case, I suspect, that the new morality will say that he is better dead. We shall each be left to pick out for ourselves whichever aunts or second cousins are better dead, and then the fun will begin. In this, as in other matters, I think we shall have either to go forward to the Utopia of massacre according to taste, or else go backward to some more solid social creed. We might begin by noting a distinction; that it is one thing to sympathise with people sorely tempted to a desperate solution, and quite another to recommend that solution. I sympathise with unhappy wives and husbands; but not so much as I do with poor pickpockets or starving brigands who kill for bread. The question is—are we to sympathise, or are we to say that it is right to steal and to stab and to destroy the institution of marriage?

The Eccentricity of Marriage[*]

In my friendly difference with Mr. Haynes,[1] he is trying
to pin me to purely sacramental and even sacerdotal questions, of whether and when a marriage may be declared to
be no marriage; whereas I have only tried, and unsuccess-
fully, to pin him to the purely secular question of whether
his own divorce schemes are likely to be a social nuisance
or not. On the question of whether any particular marriage should be annulled, as not having had its mystical
efficacy at all, I could not in any case pronounce; for this
could only logically be done by something claiming to be
a religious authority; and I do not claim to be any kind
of authority, religious or irreligious. But even such transcendental convictions as I do hold, I deliberately refrained
from introducing. In [purely] secular matters I still find the
presence of social peril.

The key of this part of Mr. Haynes' case can be found,
I take it, in the word "ideal." He suggests more than once
that he fully agrees with me in supporting the ideal of
indissoluble, or at least undissolved marriage. I am sure
that in his case this stands for a great deal of substantial
sympathy and practical support of the home, especially of
that poor home which is now so peculiarly endangered.
Unfortunately, on the theoretic side, the word "ideal" is
far from being an exact term, and is open to two almost
opposite interpretations. For many would be prepared to
say that marriage is an ideal as some would say that monas-
ticism is an ideal; in the sense of a counsel of perfection,
a rare and abnormal advantage. Now certainly we might

---

[*] Excerpt was originally published in *New Witness*, May 10, 1918.
[1] E.S.P. Haynes was a writer and lawyer who advocated more liberal
divorce laws.

preserve a conjugal ideal in this way. A man might be reverently pointed out in the street as a sort of saint, merely because he was married. A man might wear a medal for monogamy; or have letters after his name similar to V.C. or D.D.; let us say L.W. for "Lives with his Wife," or S.N.D. for "Still Not Divorced." We might, in entering some strange city, be struck by a stately column erected to the memory of a wife who never ran away with a soldier, of the shrine and image of a historical character, who had resisted the example of bolting with the children's nurse. Such high artistic hagiology would be quite consistent with Mr. Haynes' divorce reform, with re-marriage after three years, or three hours. It would also be quite consistent with Mr. Haynes' phrase about preserving an ideal of the family. What it would not be consistent with is the perfectly plain, solid, secular and social usefulness which was what I alleged to belong to the law of marriage. It would not make the average family an absolute against which misgovernment wars in vain. It would not arm the household against the tyrant as the State is armed against the foreigner. It does not ensure that whenever the unjust ruler strikes he will find, not a dust of atoms, but solid blocks of fidelity. Nothing can serve that particular purpose except a universal, or at any rate a general acceptance of the family tie, not only as an ideal but as an obligation. And I certainly do hope to safeguard all marriages, in the only sense in which a sane man can have such a hope; that is, I think the anomalous solitude or accidental temptations, of the few unhappily married or lawfully separated persons, would not be too high a price to pay for the universal power of that obligation.

Now as to the allegation that these cases are not few, or not few enough to be thus accepted, we are doubtless confronted with the whole problem of a healthier society.

On one point at least Mr. Haynes may be reassured; whatever I am defending I am not defending what he calls the *status quo* in England. I can easily believe that in this our law is an unprincipled hotchpotch; for our whole society is an unprincipled hotchpotch. And what I urge to Mr. Haynes, about the mass of the modern abuses of marriage, is what I urged about the mass of the modern abuses of drink; that in so far as their number and degree is really abnormal, it is because all the circumstances in which they exist or try to exist, are abnormal in other ways. As beer has not a fair chance among men who are denied bread, so marriage has not a fair chance among men who are denied liberty and property. And we do in fact find the same capitalist forces driving men towards a Malthusianism or an immoral celibacy as drive them towards an alternative of arsenic and cocaine.

Divorce and Slavery[*]

Divorce is a thing which the newspapers now not only advertise, but advocate, almost as if it were a pleasure in itself. It may be, indeed, that all the flowers and festivities will now be transferred from the fashionable wedding to the fashionable divorce. A superb iced and frosted divorce-cake will be provided for the feast, and in military circles will be cut with the co-respondent's sword. A dazzling display of divorce presents will be laid out for the inspection of the company, toasts will be drunk, the guests will assemble on the doorstep to see the husband and wife go off in opposite directions; and all will go merry as a

[*] Excerpt was originally published in *Illustrated London News*, September 2, 1922.

divorce-court bell. All this, though to some it might seem
a little fanciful, would really be far less fantastic than the
sort of things that are really said on the subject. I am not
going to discuss the depth and substance of that subject.
I myself hold a mystical view of marriage; but I am not
going to debate it here. But merely in the interests of light
and logic I would protest against the way in which it is
frequently debated. The process cannot rationally be called
a debate at all. It is a sort of chorus of sentimentalists in the
sensational newspapers, perpetually intoning some such
formula as this: "We respect marriage, we reverence marriage, holy, sacred, ineffably exquisite and ideal marriage.
True marriage is love, and when love alters, marriage
alters, and when love stops or begins again, marriage does
the same; wonderful, beautiful, beatific marriage."

Now, with all reasonable sympathy with everything
sentimental, I may remark that all that talk is tosh. Marriage is an institution like any other, set up deliberately to
have certain functions and limitations; it is an institution
like private property, or conscription, or the legal liberties
of the subject. To talk as if it were made or melted with
certain changing moods is a mere waste of words. The
object of private property is that as many citizens as possible should have a certain dignity and pleasure in being
masters of material things. But suppose a dog-stealer were
to say that as soon as a man was bored with his dog it
ceased to be his dog, and he ceased to be responsible for it.
Suppose he were to say that by merely coveting the dog
he could immediately morally possess the dog. The answer
would be that the only way to make men responsible for
dogs was to make the relation a legal one, apart from the
likes and dislikes of the moment. Suppose a burglar were to
say: "Private property I venerate, private property I revere;
but I am convinced that Mr. Brown does not truly value

his silver Apostle spoons as such sacred objects should be valued; they have therefore ceased to be his property; in reality they have already become my property, for I appreciate their precious character as nobody else can do." Suppose a murderer were to say: "What can be more amiable and admirable than human life lived with a due sense of its priceless opportunity! But I regret to observe that Mr. Robinson has lately been looking decidedly tired and melancholy; life accepted in this depressing and demoralising spirit can no longer truly be called life; it is rather my own exuberant and perhaps exaggerated joy of life which I must gratify by cutting his throat with a carving-knife."

It is obvious that these philosophers would fail to understand what we mean by a rule, quite apart from the problem of its exceptions. They would fail to grasp what we mean by an institution, whether it be the institution of law, of property, or of marriage. A reasonable person will certainly reply to the burglar: "You will hardly soothe us by merely poetical praises of property; because your case would be much more convincing if you denied, as the Communists do, that property ought to exist at all. There may be, there certainly are, gross abuses in private property; but, so long as it is an institution at all, it cannot alter merely with moods and emotions. A farm cannot simply float away from a farmer, in proportion as his interest in it grows fainter than it was. A house cannot shift away by inches from a householder, by certain fine shades of feeling that he happens to have about it. A dog cannot drift away like a dream, and begin to belong to somebody else who happens just then to be dreaming of him. And neither can the serious social relation of husband and wife, of mother and father, or even of man and woman, be resolved in all its relations by passions and reactions of sentiment." This question is quite apart from the question of whether there are exceptions to the rule of loyalty, or what they are. The primary point is that there is an institution to which to be loyal. If the new sentimentalists mean what they say, when they say they venerate that institution, they must not suggest that an institution can be actually identical with an emotion. And that is what their rhetoric does suggest, so far as it can be said to suggest anything.

These writers are always explaining to us why they believe in divorce. I think I can easily understand why they believe in divorce. What I do not understand is why they believe in marriage. Just as the philosophical burglar would be more philosophical if he were a Bolshevist, so this sort of divorce advocate would be more philosophical if he were a free-lover. For his arguments never seem to touch on marriage as an institution, or anything more than an individual experience. The real explanation of this strange indifference to the institutional idea is, I fancy, something not only deeper, but wider; something affecting all the institutions of the modern world. The truth is that these sociologists are not at all interested in promoting the sort of social life that marriage does promote. The sort of society of which marriage has always been the strongest pillar is what is sometimes called the distributive society; the society in which most of the citizens have a tolerable share of property, especially property in land. Everywhere, all over the world, the farm goes with the family and the family with the farm. Unless the whole domestic group hold together with a sort of loyalty or local patriotism, unless the inheritance of property is logical and legitimate, unless the family quarrels are kept out of the courts of officialism, the tradition of family ownership cannot be handed on unimpaired. On the other hand, the Servile State, which is the opposite of the distributive state, has always been rather embarrassed by the institution of marriage. It is an old story that the negro slavery of *Uncle Tom's Cabin* did its worst work in the breaking-up of families. But, curiously enough, the same story is told from both sides. For the apologists of the Slave States, or, at least, of the Southern States, make the same admission even in their own defence. If they denied breaking up the slave family, it was because they denied that there was any slave family to break up.

Free love is the direct enemy of freedom. It is the most obvious of all the bribes that can be offered by slavery. In servile societies a vast amount of sexual laxity can go on in practice, and even in theory, save when now and then some cranky speculator or crazy squire has a fad for some special breed of slaves like a breed of cattle. And even that lunacy would not last long; for lunatics are the minority among slave-owners. Slavery has a much more sane and a much more subtle appeal to human nature than that. It is much more likely that, after a few such fads and freaks, the new Servile State would settle down into the sleepy resignation of the old Servile State; the old pagan repose in slavery, as it was before Christianity came to trouble and perplex the world with ideals of liberty and chivalry. One of the conveniences of that pagan world is that, below a certain level of society, nobody really need bother about pedigree or paternity at all. A new world began when slaves began to stand on their dignity as virgin martyrs. Christendom is the civilization that such martyrs made; and slavery is its returning enemy. But of all the bribes that the old pagan slavery can offer, this luxury and laxity is the strongest; nor do I deny that the influences desiring the degradation of human dignity have here chosen their instrument well.

120

The Tragedies of Marriage[*]

The modern man wants to eat his wedding cake and have it, too.... The broadminded are extremely bitter because a Christian who wishes to have several wives when his own promise bound him to one, is not allowed to violate his vow at the same altar at which he made it. Nobody does insist on Baptists totally immersing people who totally deny the advantages of being totally immersed. Nobody ever did expect Mormons to receive the open mockers of the Book of Mormon, nor Christian Scientists to let their churches be used for exposing Mrs. Eddy as an old fraud. It is only of the forms of Christianity making the Catholic claim that such inconsistent claims are made. And even the inconsistency is, I fancy, a tribute to the acceptance of the Catholic idea in a catholic fashion.... The point here is that it is at least superficially inconsistent to ask institutions for a formal approval, which they can only give by inconsistency.

... What is divorce? It is not merely the negation or neglect of marriage; for any one can always neglect marriage. It is not the dissolution of the legal obligation of marriage, or even the legal obligation of monogamy; for the simple reason that no such obligation exists.... We cannot be forcibly introduced to a polygamist by a policeman. It would not be an assertion of social liberty, but a denial of social liberty, if we found ourselves practically obliged to associate with all the profligates in society. But divorce is not in this sense mere anarchy. On the contrary divorce is in this sense respectability; and even a rigid

*Composite essay based on excerpts from "The Tragedies of Marriage", in *CW* 4:252–61, and "The Vista of Divorce", in *The Superstition of Divorce*, in *CW* 4:272–76, 278–79, 281–82, 284, 286, 288.

excess of respectability. Divorce in this sense might indeed be not unfairly called snobbery. The definition of divorce, which concerns us here, is that it is the attempt to give respectability, and not liberty. It is the attempt to give a certain social status, and not a legal status. It is indeed supposed that this can be done by the alteration of certain legal forms; and this will be more or less true according to the extent to which law as such overawed public opinion, or was valued as a true expression of public opinion.... But the peculiar point here is that many are claiming the sanction of religion as well as of respectability. They would attach to their very natural and sometimes very pardonable experiments a certain atmosphere, and even glamour, which has undoubtedly belonged to the status of marriage in historic Christendom. But before they make this attempt, it would be well to ask why such a dignity ever appeared or in what it consisted. And I fancy we shall find ourselves confronted with the very simple truth, that the dignity arose wholly and entirely out of the fidelity; and that the glamour merely came from the vow. People were regarded as having a certain dignity because they were dedicated in a certain way; as bound to certain duties and, if it be preferred, to certain discomforts. It may be irrational to endure these discomforts; it may even be irrational to respect them. But it is certainly much more irrational to respect them, and then artificially transfer the same respect to the absence of them....

What is respected, in short, is the fidelity to the ancient flag of the family, and a readiness to fight for what I have noted as its unique type of freedom. I say readiness to fight, for fortunately the fight itself is the exception rather than the rule. The soldier is not respected because he is doomed to death, but because he is ready for death; and even ready for defeat. The married man or woman is not doomed to evil, sickness or poverty; but is respected for taking a certain step for better for worse, for richer for poorer, in sickness or in health. But there is one result of this line of argument which should correct a danger in some arguments on the same side.

It is very essential that a stricture on divorce, which is in fact simply a defence of marriage, should be independent of sentimentalism, especially in the form called optimism. A man justifying a fight for national independence or civic freedom is neither sentimental nor optimistic. He explains the sacrifice, but he does not explain it away.... However beautiful you may think your own visions of beatitude, men must suffer to be beautiful, and even suffer a considerable interval of being ugly. And I have no notion of denying that mankind suffers much from the maintenance of the standard of marriage; as it suffers much from the necessity of criminal law or the recurrence of crusades and revolutions. The only question here is whether marriage is indeed, as I maintain, an ideal and an institution making for popular freedom; I do not need to be told that anything making for popular freedom has to be paid for in vigilance and pain, and a whole army of martyrs.

Hence I am far indeed from denying the hard cases which exist here, as in all matters involving the idea of honour. But it will be well to discuss in a little more detail what are described as the tragedies of marriage. And the first thing to note about the most tragic of them is that they are not tragedies of marriage at all. They are tragedies of sex; and might easily occur in a highly modern romance in which marriage was not mentioned at all. It is generally summarised by saying that the tragic element is the absence of love. But it is often forgotten that another tragic element is often the presence of love. The doctors of divorce, with an air of the frank and friendly realism of men of the world, are always recommending and rejoicing in a sensible separation by mutual consent. But if we are really to dismiss our dreams of dignity and honour, if we are really to fall back on the frank realism of our experience as men of the world, then the very first thing that our experience will tell us is that it very seldom is a separation by mutual consent; that is, that the consent very seldom is sincerely and spontaneously mutual. By far the commonest problem in such cases is that in which one party wishes to end the partnership and the other does not. And of that emotional situation you can make nothing but a tragedy, whichever way you turn it. With or without marriage, with or without divorce, with or without any arrangements that anybody can suggest or imagine, it remains a tragedy. The only difference is that by the doctrine of marriage it remains both a noble and a fruitful tragedy; like that of a man who falls fighting for his country, or dies testifying to the truth. But the truth is that the innovators have as much sham optimism about divorce as any romanticist can have had about marriage. They regard their story, when it ends in the divorce court, through as rosy a mist of sentimentalism as anybody ever regarded a story ending with wedding bells. Such a reformer is quite sure that when once the prince and princess are divorced by the fairy godmother, they will live happily ever after. I enjoy romance, but I like it to be rooted in reality; and any one with a touch of reality knows that nine couples out of ten, when they are divorced, are left in an exceedingly different state. It will be safe to say in most cases that one partner will fail to find happiness in an infatuation, and the other will from the first accept a tragedy. In the realm of reality and not romance, it is commonly a case of breaking hearts as well as breaking promises; and even dishonour is not always a remedy for remorse....

To put it roughly, we are prepared in some cases to listen to the man who complains of having a wife. But we are not prepared to listen, at such length, to the same man when he comes back and complains that he has not got a wife. Now in practice at this moment the great mass of the complaints are precisely of this kind. The reformers insist particularly on the pathos of a man's position when he has obtained a separation without a divorce. Their most tragic figure is that of the man who is already free of all those ills he had, and is only asking to be allowed to fly to others that he knows not of. I should be the last to deny that, in certain emotional circumstances, his tragedy may be very tragic indeed. But his tragedy is of the emotional kind which can never be entirely eliminated; and which he has himself, in all probability, inflicted on the partner he has left.... The battle joins on the debatable ground, not of the man's doubtful past but of his still more doubtful future. In a word, the divorce controversy is not really a controversy about divorce. It is a controversy about re-marriage; or rather about whether it is marriage at all....

The case for divorce combines all the advantages of having it both ways; and of drawing the same deduction from right or left, and from black or white. Whichever way the programme works in practice, it can still be justified in theory. If there are few examples of divorce, it shows how little divorce need be dreaded; if there are many, it shows how much it is required. The rarity of divorce is an argument in favor of divorce; and the multiplicity of divorce is an argument against marriage. Now, in truth, if we were confined to considering this alternative in a speculative manner, if there were no concrete facts but only abstract probabilities, we should have no difficulty in arguing our case. The abstract liberty allowed by the reformers is as near as possible to anarchy, and gives no logical or legal guarantee worth discussing. The advantages of their reform do not accrue to the innocent party, but to the guilty party; especially if he be sufficiently guilty. A man has only to commit the crime of desertion to obtain the reward of divorce.... The point of divorce reform, it cannot be too often repeated, is that the rascal should not only be regarded as romantic, but regarded as respectable. He is not to sow his wild oats and settle down; he is merely to settle down to sowing his wild oats. They are to be regarded as tame and inoffensive oats; almost, if one may say so, as Quaker oats. But there is no need, as I say, to speculate about whether the looser view of divorce might prevail; for it is already prevailing. The newspapers are full of an astonishing hilarity about the rapidity with which hundreds or thousands of human families are being broken up by the lawyers....

In face of this headlong fashion, it is really reasonable to ask the divorce reformers what is their attitude towards the old monogamous ethic of our civilisation; and whether they wish to retain it in general, or to retain it at all....

... The obvious effect of frivolous divorce will be frivolous marriage. If people can be separated for no reason they will feel it all the easier to be united for no reason. A man might quite clearly foresee that a sensual infatuation would be fleeting, and console himself with the knowledge that the connection could be equally fleeting....

Anarchy cannot last, but anarchic communities cannot last either. Mere lawlessness cannot live, but it can destroy life. The nations of the earth always return to sanity and solidarity; but the nations which return to it first are the nations which survive....

... It is the more complex types of society that are now entangled in their own complexities. Those who tell us, with a monotonous metaphor, that we cannot put the clock back, seem to be curiously unconscious of the fact that their own clock has stopped. And there is nothing so hopeless as clockwork when it stops. A machine cannot mend itself, it requires a man to mend it; and the future lies with those who can make living laws for men and not merely dead laws for machinery. Those living laws are not to found in the scatterbrained scepticism which is busy in the great cities, dissolving what it cannot analyse. The primary laws of man are to be found in the permanent life of man; in those things that have been common to it in every time and land, though in the highest civilisation they have reached an enrichment like that of the divine romance of Cana in Galilee. We know that many critics of such a story say that its elements are not permanent; but indeed it is the critics who are not permanent. A hundred mad dogs of heresy have worried man from the beginning; but it was always the dog that died. We know there is a school of prigs who disapprove of the wine; and there may now be a school of prigs who disapprove of the wedding. For in such a case as the story of Cana, it may be remarked that the pedants are prejudiced against the earthly elements as much as, or more than, the heavenly elements. It is not the supernatural that disgusts them, so much as the natural. And those of us who have seen all the normal rules and relations of humanity uprooted by random speculators, as if they were abnormal abuses and almost accidents, will understand why men have sought for something divine if they wished to preserve anything human. They will know why common sense, cast out from some academy of fads and fashions conducted on the lines of a luxurious mad-house, has age after age sought refuge in the high sanity of a sacrament.

Mr. and Mrs. Macbeth[*]

The good old habit of murdering kings (which was the salvation of so many commonwealths in the past) has fallen into desuetude. The idea of such a play must be for us (and for our sins) more subtle. The idea is more subtle but it is almost inexpressibly great. Let us before reading the play consider if only for a moment what is the main idea of *Macbeth* for modern men.

One great idea on which all tragedy builds is the idea of the continuity of human life. The one thing a man cannot do is exactly what all modern artists and free lovers are always trying to do. He cannot cut his life up into separate sections. The case of the modern claim for freedom in love is the first and most obvious that occurs to the mind; therefore I use it for this purpose of illustration. You can-not have an idyll with Maria and an episode with Jane; there is no such thing as an episode. There is no such thing as an idyll. It is idle to talk about abolishing the tragedy of marriage when you cannot abolish the tragedy of sex. Every flirtation is a marriage; it is a marriage in this fright-ful sense; that it is irrevocable. I have taken this case of sexual relations as one out of a hundred; but of any case in human life the thing is true. The basis of all tragedy is that man lives a coherent and continuous life. It is only a worm

---

[*] Excerpt from "The Macbeths", in *The Soul of Wit: G. K. Chesterton on William Shakespeare*, ed. Dale Ahlquist (Mineola, NY: Dover, 2012), pp. 74–82. Reprinted by permission.

that you can cut in two and leave the severed parts still alive. You can cut a worm up into episodes and they are still living episodes. You can cut a worm up into idylls and they are quite brisk and lively idylls. You can do all this to him precisely because he is a worm. You cannot cut a man up and leave him kicking, precisely because he is a man. We know this because man even in his lowest and darkest manifestation has always this characteristic of physical and psychological unity. His identity continues long enough to see the end of many of his own acts; he cannot be cut off from his past with a hatchet; as he sows so shall he reap.

This then is the basis of all tragedy, this living and perilous continuity which does not exist in the lower creatures. This is the basis of all tragedy, and this is certainly the basis of *Macbeth*.

The great ideas of *Macbeth*, uttered in the first few scenes with a tragic energy which has never been equalled perhaps in Shakespeare or out of him, is the idea of the enormous mistake a man makes if he supposes that one decisive act will clear his way. Macbeth's ambition, though selfish and someway sullen, is not in itself criminal or morbid. He wins the title of Glamis in honourable war; he deserves and gets the title of Cawdor; he is rising in the world and has a not ignoble exhilaration in doing so. Suddenly a new ambition is presented to him (of the agency and atmosphere which presents it I shall speak in a moment) and he realizes that nothing lies across his path to the Crown of Scotland except the sleeping body of Duncan. If he does that one cruel thing, he can be infinitely kind and happy.

Here, I say, is the first and most formidable of the great actualities of *Macbeth*. You cannot do a mad thing in order to reach sanity. Macbeth's mad resolve is not a cure even for his own irresolution. He was indecisive before his decision. He is, if possible, more indecisive after he has decided. The crime does not get rid of the problem. Its effect is so bewildering that one may say that the crime does not get rid of the temptation. Make a morbid decision and you will only become more morbid; do a lawless thing and you will only get into an atmosphere much more suffocating than that of law. Indeed, it is a mistake to speak of a man as "breaking out." The lawless man never breaks out; he breaks in. He smashes a door and finds himself in another room, he smashes a wall and finds himself in a yet smaller one. The more he shatters the more his habitation shrinks. Where he ends you may read in the end of *Macbeth*.

For us moderns, therefore, the first philosophical significance of the play is this; that our life is one thing and that our lawless acts limit us; every time we break a law we make a limitation. In some strange way hidden in the deeps of human psychology, if we build our palace on some unknown wrong it turns very slowly into our prison. Macbeth at the end of the play is not merely a wild beast; he is a caged wild beast. But if this is the thing to be put in a primary position there is something else that demands at least our second one. The second idea in the main story of *Macbeth* is, of course, that of the influence of evil suggestion upon the soul, particularly evil suggestion of a mystical and transcendental kind. In this connection the mystical character of the promptings is not more interesting than the mystical character of the man to whom they are especially sent. Mystical promptings are naturally sweet to a mystic. The character of Macbeth in this regard has been made the matter of a great deal of brilliant and futile discussion. Some critics have represented him as a burly silent soldier because he won battles for his country. Other critics have represented him as a feverish and futile decadent because he makes long practical speeches full of the most elaborate imagery. In the name of commonsense let it be remembered that Shakespeare lived before the time when unsuccessful poets thought it poetical to be decadent and unsuccessful soldiers thought it military to be silent. Men like Sidney and Raleigh and Essex could have fought as well as Macbeth and could have ranted as well as Macbeth. Why should Shakespeare shrink from making a great general talk poetry when half the great generals of his time actually wrote great poetry?

The whole legend, therefore, which some critics have based on the rich rhetoric of *Macbeth*: the legend that Macbeth was a febrile and egotistical coward because he liked the sound of his own voice, may be dismissed as a manifestation of the diseases of later days. Shakespeare meant Macbeth for a fine orator for he made fine speeches; he also meant him for a fine soldier because he made him not only win battles bravely but what is much more to the point, lose battles bravely; he made him, when overwhelmed by enemies in heaven and earth, die the death of a hero. But Macbeth is meant to be among other things an orator and a poet; and it is to Macbeth in this capacity that the evil supernatural appeal is made. If there be any such thing as evil influences coming from beyond the world, they have never been so suggestively indicated as they are here. They appeal, as evil always does, to the existence of a coherent and comprehensible scheme. It is the essence of a nightmare that it turns the whole cosmos against us. Two of their prophecies have been fulfilled; may it not be assumed then that the third will also be fulfilled?

Also they appeal, as evil always does (being slavish itself and believing all men slaves) to the inevitable. They put Macbeth's good fortune before him as if it were not so much a fortune as a fate. In the same way imperialists sought to salve the consciences of Englishmen by giving them the offer of gold and empire with all the gloom of predestination. When the devil, and the witches who are the servants of the devil, wish to make a weak man snatch a crown that does not belong to him, they are too cunning to come to him and say "Will you be King?" They say without further parley, "All hail, Macbeth, that shall be king hereafter". This weakness Macbeth really has; that he is easily attracted by that kind of spiritual fatalism which relieves the human creature of a great part of his responsibility. In this way there is a strange and sinister appropriateness in the way in which the promises of the evil spirits end in new fantasies; end, so to speak, as mere diabolical jokes. Macbeth accepts as a piece of unreasoning fate first his crime and then his crown. It is appropriate that this fate which he has accepted as external and irrational should end in incidents of mere extravagant bathos, in the walking forest and strange birth of Macduff. He has once surrendered himself with a kind of dark and evil faith, to a machinery of destiny that he can neither respect nor understand, and it is the proper sequel of this that the machinery should produce a situation which crushes him as something useless.

Shakespeare does not mean that Macbeth's emotionalism and rich rhetoric prove him to be unmanly in any ordinary sense. But Shakespeare does mean, I think, to suggest that the man, virile in his essential structure, has this weak spot in his artistic temperament; that fear of the mere strength of destiny and of unknown spirits, of their strength as apart from their virtue, which is the only proper significance of the word superstition. No man can be superstitious who loves his God, even if the god be Mumbo-Jumbo. Macbeth has something of this fear and fatalism; and fatalism is exactly the point at which rationalism passes silently into superstition. Macbeth, in short, has any amount of physical courage, he has even a great deal of moral courage. But he lacks what may be called spiritual courage; he lacks a certain freedom and dignity of the human soul in the universe, a freedom and dignity which one of the scriptural writers expresses as the difference between the servants and the sons of God.

But the man Macbeth and his marked but inadequate manliness, can only be expressed in connection with the character of his wife. And the question of Lady Macbeth immediately arouses again the controversies that have surrounded this play. The question as commonly stated, in short, is the question of whether Macbeth was really masculine, and second, of whether Lady Macbeth was not really feminine. The old critics assumed that because Lady Macbeth obviously ruled her husband she must have been a masculine woman. The whole inference of course is false. Masculine women may rule the Borough Council, but they never rule their husbands. The women who rule their husbands are the feminine women and I am entirely in accord with those who think that Lady Macbeth must have been a very feminine woman. But while some critics rightly insist on the feminine character of Lady Macbeth they endeavour to deprive Macbeth of that masculine character which is obviously the corollary of the other. They think Lady Macbeth must be a man because she rules. And on the same idiotic principle they think that Macbeth must be a woman or a coward or a decadent or something odd because he is ruled. The most masculine kind of man always is ruled. As a friend of mine once said, very truly, physical cowards are the only men who are not afraid of women.

The real truth about Macbeth and his wife is somewhat strange but cannot be too strongly stated. Nowhere else in all his wonderful works did Shakespeare describe the real character of the relations of the sexes so sanely, or so satisfactorily as he describes it here. The man and the woman are never more normal than they are in this abnormal and horrible story. *Romeo and Juliet* does not better describe love than this describes marriage. The dispute that goes on between Macbeth and his wife about the murder of Duncan is almost word for word a dispute which goes on at any suburban breakfast-table about something else. It is merely a matter of changing "Infirm of purpose, give me the daggers", into "infirm of purpose, give me the postage stamps". And it is quite a mistake to suppose that the woman is to be called masculine or even in any exclusive sense strong. The strengths of the two partners differ in kind. The woman has more of that strength on the spot which is called industry. The man has more of that strength in reserve which is called laziness.

But the acute truth of this actual relation is much deeper even than that. Lady Macbeth exhibits one queer and astounding kind of magnanimity which is quite peculiar to women. That is, she will take something that her husband dares not do but which she knows he wants to do and she will become more fierce for it than he is. For her, as for all very feminine souls (that is, very strong ones) selfishness is the only thing which is acutely felt as sin; she will commit any crime if she is not committing it only for herself. Her husband thirsts for the crime egotistically and therefore vaguely, darkly, and subconsciously, as a man becomes conscious of the beginnings of physical thirst. But she thirsts for the crime altruistically and therefore clearly and sharply, as a man perceives a public duty to society. She puts the thing in plain words, with an acceptance of extremes. She has that perfect and splendid cynicism of women which is the most terrible thing God has made. I say it without irony and without any undue enjoyment of the slight element of humour.

If you want to know what are the permanent relations of the married man with the married woman you cannot read it anywhere more accurately than in the little domestic idyll of Mr. and Mrs. Macbeth. Of a man so male and a woman so female, I cannot believe anything except that they ultimately save their souls. Macbeth was strong in every masculine sense up to the very last moment; he killed himself in battle. Lady Macbeth was strong in the very female sense which is perhaps a more courageous sense; she killed herself, but not in battle. As I say, I cannot think that souls so strong and so elemental have not retained those permanent possibilities of humility and gratitude which ultimately place the soul in heaven. But wherever they are they are together. For alone among so many of the figures of human fiction, they are actually married.

4

Babies ... and Birth Control

By the Babe Unborn

If all the sky were full of stars
And all the hills of grass,
And all the roofs of chimney-pots
How well the time would pass.

If there were streets where folk went by
And fields where flowers grew
And roads ran up against the hill
I know what I shall do.

I think that if they gave me leave
Within that world to stand
I would be good for all the day,
I spent in fairyland.

They should not hear a word from me
Of selfishness or scorn
If only I could find the way,
If only I were born.

Birthdays are a glorification of the idea of life.

— *Illustrated London News*, November 28, 1908

A man's birthday reminds him that he is alive, when his immediate affairs would only remind him that he was at work or at play, in business or in debt.

— *New Witness*, August 9, 1918

There is a sense in which I am so much astonished at being
alive that I cannot be astonished at anything afterwards....
A man who truly realized, for an instant, that he is still
alive, might almost die of the shock.

— *New Witness*, May 16, 1919

Life is serious all the time; but living cannot be serious
all the time.... In anything that does cover the whole of
your life—in your philosophy and your religion—you
must have mirth. If you do not have mirth you will certainly have madness.

— *Daily News*, September 1, 1906

All precious things [are] in perpetual and incurable peril.

— *Speaker*, January 14, 1905

Every high civilization decays by forgetting obvious things.

— "The Way of the Desert",
The New Jerusalem

Our generation, in a dirty, pessimistic period, has blasphe-
mously underrated the beauty of life and cravenly over-
rated its dangers.

— *Illustrated London News*, May 30, 1908

The only object of liberty is life.

— "Belfast and the Religious Problem",
Irish Impressions

How can it be more important to teach a child how to
avoid disease than how to value life?

— *Daily News*, April 28, 1906

There was a dramatic drop in moral standards on the day they discovered that the test-tube is mightier than the sword.

> —*Illustrated London News*, March 4, 1916

A strange fanaticism fills our time: the fanatical hatred of morality, especially of Christian morality.

> —"The Moral Philosophy of Meredith",
> *A Handful of Authors*

The moment sex ceases to be a servant it becomes a tyrant.

> —"The World St. Francis Found", *St. Francis of Assisi*

Contraception ... stalks through the modern State, leading the march of human progress through abortion to infanticide.

> —"Where Is Paradox", *The Well and the Shallows*

Abortion is ... the mutilation of womanhood and the massacre of men unborn.

> —"The Meanness of the Motive",
> *Eugenics and Other Evils*

As the Christ Child could be hidden from Herod—so the child unborn is still hidden from the omniscient oppressor ... and they seek his life to take it away.

> —"The True History of a Tramp",
> *Eugenics and Other Evils*

Eugenics is chiefly a denial of the Declaration of Independence. It urges that so far from all men being born equal, numbers of them ought not to be born all.

> —*Illustrated London News*, November 20, 1915

I might inform those humanitarians who have a nightmare of new and needless babies (for some humanitarians have that sort of horror of humanity) that if the recent decline in the birth-rate were continued for a certain time, it might end in there being no babies at all; which would console them very much.

— *Illustrated London News*, May 24, 1930

If there is no authority in things which Christendom has called moral, because their origins were mystical, then they are clearly free to ignore all difference between animals and men; and treat men as we treat animals.... Let all the babies be born; and then let us drown those we do not like.

— "Babies and Distributism",
The Well and the Shallows

Wherever there is Animal Worship there is Human Sacrifice.

— *Illustrated London News*, January 17, 1914

We naturally expect that the protest against that more than usually barbaric form of birth control will be a protest of indignant instinct and the common conscience of men. We expect the infanticide to be called by its own name, which is murder at its worst; not only the brand of Cain but the brand of Herod. We expect the protest to be full of the honour of men, of the memory of mothers, of the natural love of children.

— *Illustrated London News*, June 3, 1922

Now, the Carthaginians were a highly civilised and even refined people, whose religion largely consisted of burning alive a large number of children as a sacrifice to Moloch....

Moloch is not fallen; Moloch is in his high place, and his furnaces consume mankind; his armies overrun the earth, and his ships threaten our own island. The question on the lips of any living man is not whether some who burn their children may nevertheless love their children, it is whether those who burn their children shall conquer those who don't. The parallel is practically quite justifiable; what we are fighting has all the regularity of a horrible religion. We are not at war with regrettable incidents or sad exceptions, but with a system like the system of sacrificing babies; a system of drowning neutrals, a system of enslaving civilians, a system of attacking hospital services, a system of exterminating chivalry.

> — *Illustrated London News*, December 29, 1923;
> July 20, 1918

God Himself will not help us to ignore evil, but only to defy and to defeat it.

> — *Illustrated London News*, April 14, 1917

Unless a man becomes an enemy of such an evil, he will not even become its slave, but rather its champion.

> — *Illustrated London News*, April 14, 1917

Nearly all newspapers and public speakers now are entirely occupied with finding harmless words for a horrible thing.

> — *G. K.'s Weekly*, October 17, 1931

Throughout numberless ages and nations, the normal and real birth control is called self control.... But the thing the capitalist newspapers call birth control is not control at all. It is the idea that people should be, in one respect, completely and utterly uncontrolled, so long as they can evade everything in the function that is positive and creative,

and intelligent and worthy of a free man. It is a name
given to a succession of different expedients (the one that
was used last is always described as having been dreadfully
dangerous) by which it is possible to filch the pleasure
belonging to a natural process while violently and unnaturally thwarting the process itself.

— "Social Reform vs. Birth Control",
in pamphlet, 1927

This is ... the sort of plunging and premature pessimism
... that people exhibit about Birth Control. Their desire is
towards destruction; their hope is for despair; they eagerly
anticipate the darkest and most doubtful predictions.

— "The Need of a New Spirit",
The Outline of Sanity

As social reform goes forward ... it will be found easy to
decree (in order to save the overwhelming over-work of
the panel doctor) that insured persons shall only have so
many children; and that the extra babies shall be abolished
beforehand by the Birth Control expert, or afterwards by
the lethal chamber.

— *G. K.'s Weekly*, July 16, 1927

We are not so very far off even the sacrifice of babies....
I have seen versions of eugenics that come very near to
infanticide.

— *Illustrated London News*, December 4, 1920

The most unfathomable schools and sages have never
attained to the gravity which dwells in the eyes of a baby
of three months old. It is the gravity of astonishment at
the universe.

— "In Defence of Baby Worship", *The Defendant*

Men live ... rejoicing from age to age in something fresher than progress—in the fact that with every baby a new sun and a new moon are made.

—"The Two Voices", *The Napoleon of Notting Hill*

A literary man who cannot see that a baby is marvelous could not see that anything was marvelous.

—*Illustrated London News*, March 7, 1931

The whole difference between construction and creation is exactly this: that a thing constructed can only be loved after it is constructed; but a thing created is loved before it exists, as the mother can love the unborn child.

—"Pickwick Papers", *Appreciations and Criticisms of the Works of Charles Dickens*

Christianity, which has been ludicrously accused of being gloomy and the enemy of life, has distinguished itself among the creeds of the world by its quite peculiar insistence on the fact that life is sacred, even when it is sad; that a man is sacred, even when he is oneself.

—*Daily News*, September 17, 1904

Everybody knows what birth control means. It means love towards sex that is *not* towards life.

—*G.K.'s Weekly*, March 28, 1925

The genealogical tree is really a most common or garden sort of tree. It is only the tree of life; a mere trifle. The feeling of interest in one's own family is one of the most natural and universal feelings; it has nothing particularly oligarchical, or even aristocratic about it. And when the philosophers discovered that all men were important, they ought obviously to have discovered that all families were important.

—*Illustrated London News*, January 1, 1921

We are more hopeful for human families, and their power of finding happiness, than are the Birth-Preventionists; we may be mistaken, but we cannot be morbid. Yet they cannot even talk of us except in terms of morbidity. The truth is that the morbidity and the pessimism are all on their side and not on ours, and this ... applies to political as well as moral ideas. We believe in liberty more than they do; in love more than they do; in local common sense more than they do; and we are therefore consistent in more often trusting abnormal children to their normal families; or thinking that most people would be happier with families than without. We have the same attitude to the idea of trusting the common people with private property and political liberty. And our chief enemy is the "ascetical element" in the scientists and sociologists, who have really no notions except the negative ones of amputation and annihilation.

— *G. K.'s Weekly*, February 1, 1934

All primary liberties are perilous because they are primary. To say that a thing is a vital need is the same as saying it is a mortal need. It is saying, in the exact sense, that it is a matter of life and death. The closer we come to domestic things the closer we come to danger; for human beings are still generally born at home and still generally die at home. Days may come of a broader and more benevolent bureaucracy, when everybody will be born in a hospital and everybody will die in a work-house. Under such scientific supervision, however, I am by no means certain that fewer will die; and I have heard some scientific assurances that fewer will be born.

— *New Witness*, December 31, 1920

The present tendency of social reform would seem to consist of destroying all traces of the parents.

— "The Family and the Feud", *Irish Impressions*

The people reading what is called the Popular Press are now treated as if they were all babies: perhaps to balance the absence of real babies in the Birth Statistics.

— *G. K.'s Weekly*, February 7, 1935

Democracy is now much discredited largely because its basic ideal of brotherhood has become merely a *metaphor*. And why? Because fewer families know what is meant by "brothers." In other words, large families train the young in an experience of equals. Solitary children know only superiors.

— *Manchester Evening News*, May 8, 1936

Hygiene may any day enforce the pagan habit of cremation. Eugenics is already hinting at infanticide. The next adventure in the long story of the strange sect called Christians may be to be asked once more to worship the god of Government; to be told once more to offer incense to Divine Caesar.

— *Dublin Review*, October–December 1910

There are more ways than one of committing infanticide; and one way is to murder the infancy without murdering the infant.

— "Rhymes for Children", *GKC as MC*

People would better understand the popular fury against the witches if they remembered that the malice most commonly attributed to them was preventing the birth of children.

— "The Demons and the Philosophers",
The Everlasting Man

When somebody wishes to wage a social war against what all normal people have regarded as a social decency, the very first thing he does is to find some artificial term that shall sound relatively decent.

—Illustrated London News, June 30, 1928

Nobody seems to see the point about the peril of scientific legislation, as in experiments by the Ministry of Health and similar things. Of course, scientific politics only means popular science. Or rather, it means politician's science, which is worse.

—Illustrated London News, March 17, 1923

I have often wondered how the scientific Marxians and the believers in "the materialist view of history" will ever manage to teach their dreary economic generalizations to children: but I suppose they will have no children.

— "Child's History of England", *Appreciations and Criticisms of the Works of Charles Dickens*

A Defence of Baby-Worship[*]

The two facts which attract almost every normal person to children are, first, that they are very serious, and, secondly, that they are in consequence very happy. They are jolly with the completeness which is possible only in the absence of humour. The most unfathomable schools and sages have never attained to the gravity which dwells in the eyes of a baby of three months old. It is the gravity of astonishment at the universe, and astonishment at the universe is not mysticism, but a transcendent common-sense.

[*] "A Defence of Baby-Worship", in *The Defendant* (New York: Dodd, Mead & Co., 1904), pp. 112–17.

The fascination of children lies in this: that with each of them all things are remade, and the universe is put again upon its trial. As we walk the streets and see below us those delightful bulbous heads, three times too big for the body, which mark these human mushrooms, we ought always primarily to remember that within every one of these heads there is a new universe, as new as it was on the seventh day of creation. In each of those orbs there is a new system of stars, new grass, new cities, a new sea.

There is always in the healthy mind an obscure prompting that religion teaches us rather to dig than to climb; that if we could once understand the common clay of earth we should understand everything. Similarly, we have the sentiment that if we could destroy custom at a blow and see the stars as a child sees them, we should need no other apocalypse. This is the great truth which has always lain at the back of baby-worship, and which will support it to the end. Maturity, with its endless energies and aspirations, may easily be convinced that it will find new things to appreciate; but it will never be convinced, at bottom, that it has properly appreciated what it has got. We may scale the heavens and find new stars innumerable, but there is still the new star we have not found—that on which we were born.

But the influence of children goes further than its first trifling effort of remaking heaven and earth. It forces us actually to remodel our conduct in accordance with this revolutionary theory of the marvellousness of all things. We do (even when we are perfectly simple or ignorant)—we do actually treat talking in children as marvellous, walking in children as marvellous, common intelligence in children as marvellous. The cynical Philosopher fancies he has a victory in this matter—that he can laugh when he shows that the words or antics of the child, so much admired by its worshippers, are common enough. The fact is that this is precisely where baby-worship is so profoundly right. Any words and any antics in a lump of clay are wonderful, the child's words and antics are wonderful, and it is only fair to say that the philosopher's words and antics are equally wonderful.

The truth is that it is our attitude towards children that is right, and our attitude towards grown-up people that is wrong. Our attitude towards our equals in age consists in a servile solemnity, overlying a considerable degree of indifference or disdain. Our attitude towards children consists in a condescending indulgence, overlying an unfathomable respect. We bow to grown people, take off our hats to them, refrain from contradicting them flatly, but we do not appreciate them properly. We make puppets of children, lecture them, pull their hair, and reverence, love, and fear them. When we reverence anything in the mature, it is their virtues or their wisdom, and this is an easy matter. But we reverence the faults and follies of children.

We should probably come considerably nearer to the true conception of things if we treated all grown-up persons, of all titles and types, with precisely that dark affection and dazed respect with which we treat the infantile limitations. A child has a difficulty in achieving the miracle of speech, consequently we find his blunders almost as marvellous as his accuracy. If we only adopted the same attitude towards Premiers and Chancellors of the Exchequer, if we genially encouraged their stammering and delightful attempts at human speech, we should be in a far more wise and tolerant temper. A child has a knack of making experiments in life, generally healthy in motive, but often intolerable in a domestic commonwealth. If we only treated all commercial buccaneers and bumptious tyrants on the same terms, if we gently chided their brutalities as rather quaint mistakes in the conduct of life, if we simply told them that they would "understand when they were older," we should probably be adopting the best and most crushing attitude towards the weaknesses of humanity. In our relations to children we prove that the paradox is entirely true, that it is possible to combine an amnesty that verges on contempt with a worship that verges upon terror. We forgive children with the same kind of blasphemous gentleness with which Omar Khayyam forgave the Omnipotent.

The essential rectitude of our view of children lies in the fact that we feel them and their ways to be supernatural while, for some mysterious reason, we do not feel ourselves or our own ways to be supernatural. The very smallness of children makes it possible to regard them as marvels; we seem to be dealing with a new race, only to be seen through a microscope. I doubt if anyone of any tenderness or imagination can see the hand of a child and not be a little frightened of it. It is awful to think of the essential human energy moving so tiny a thing; it is like imagining that human nature could live in the wing of a butterfly or the leaf of a tree. When we look upon lives so human and yet so small, we feel as if we ourselves were enlarged to an embarrassing bigness of stature. We feel the same kind of obligation to these creatures that a deity might feel if he had created something that he could not understand.

But the humorous look of children is perhaps the most endearing of all the bonds that hold the Cosmos together. Their top-heavy dignity is more touching than any humility; their solemnity gives us more hope for all things than a thousand carnivals of optimism; their large and lustrous eyes seem to hold all the stars in their astonishment; their fascinating absence of nose seems to give to us the most perfect hint of the humour that awaits us in the kingdom of heaven.

148

Three Foes of the Family[*]

It was certainly a very brilliant lightning flash of irony, by which Mr. Aldous Huxley lit up the whole loathsome landscape of his satirical Utopia, of synthetic humanity and manufactured men and women, by the old romantic quotation of "Brave New World." The quotation comes, of course, from that supreme moment of the magic of youth, nourished by the magic of old age, when Miranda the marvellous becomes Miranda the marvelling, at the unique wonder of first love. To use it for the very motto of a system which, having lost all innocence, would necessarily lose all wonder, was a touch of very withering wit. And yet it will be well to remember that, in comparison with some other worlds, where the same work is done more weakly and quite as wickedly, the Utopia of the extremists really has something of the intellectual integrity which belongs to extremes, even of madness. In that sense the two ironical adjectives are not merely ironical. The horrible human, or inhuman, hive described in Mr. Huxley's romance is certainly a base world, and a filthy world, and a fundamentally unhappy world. But it is in one sense a new world; and it is in one sense a brave world. At least a certain amount of bravery, as well as brutality, would have to be shown before anything of the sort could be established in the world of fact. It would need some courage, and even some self-sacrifice, to establish anything so utterly disgusting as that.

But the same work is being done in other worlds that are not particularly new, and not in the least brave. There are people of another sort, much more common and conventional, who are not only working to create such a paradise

* "Three Foes of the Family", in *The Well and the Shallows*, in *CW* 3:442–44.

of cowardice, but who actually try to work for it through a conspiracy of cowards. The attitude of these people towards the Family and the tradition of its Christian virtues is the attitude of men willing to wound and yet afraid to strike; or ready to sap and mine so long as they are not called upon to fire or fight in the open. And those who do this cover much more than half, or nearly two-thirds, of the people who write the most respectable and conventional Capitalist newspapers, from Punch to the News-Chronicle. It cannot be too often repeated that what destroyed the Family in the modern world was Capitalism. No doubt, it might have been Communism, if Communism had ever had a chance, outside that semi-Mongolian wilderness where it actually flourishes. But, so far as we are concerned, what has broken up households, and encouraged divorces, and treated the old domestic virtues with more and more open contempt, is the epoch and power of Capitalism. It is Capitalism that has forced a moral feud and a commercial competition between the sexes; that has destroyed the influence of the parents in favour of the influence of the employer; that has driven men from their homes to look for jobs; that has forced them to live near their factories or their firms instead of near their families; and, above all, that has encouraged, for commercial reasons, a parade of publicity and garish novelty, which is in its nature the death of all that was called dignity and modesty by our mothers and fathers. It is not the Bolshevist but the Boss, the publicity man, the salesman and the commercial advertiser who have, like a rush and riot of barbarians, thrown down and trampled under foot the ancient Roman statue of Verecundia. But because the thing is done by men of this sort, of course it is done in their own muggy and muddleheaded way; by all the irresponsible tricks of their foul Suggestion and their filthy Psychology. It is done, for instance, by perpetually guying the old Victorian virtues or limitations which, as they are no longer there, are not likely to retaliate. It is done more by pictures than by printed words; because printed words are supposed to make some sense and a man may be answerable for printing them. Stiff and hideous effigies of women in crinolines or bonnets are paraded, as if that could possibly be all there was to see when Maud came into the garden, and was saluted by such a song. Fortunately Maud's friends, who would have challenged the pressman and photographer to a duel, are all dead; and these satirists of Victorianism are very careful to find out that all their enemies are dead. Some of their bold caricaturists have been known to charge an old-fashioned bathing-machine as courageously as if it were a machine-gun. It is convenient thus courageously to attack bathing-machines, because there are no bathing machines to attack. Then they balance these things by photographs of the Modern Girl at various stages of the nudist movement; and trust that anything so obviously vulgar is bound to be popular. For the rest, the Modern Girl is floated on a sea of sentimental sloppiness; a continuous gush about her frankness and freshness, the perfect naturalness of her painting her face or the unprecedented courage of her having no children. The whole is diluted with a dreary hypocrisy about comradeship, far more sentimental than the old-fashioned sentiment. When I see the Family sinking in these swamps of amorphous amorous futility, I feel inclined to say, "Give me the Communists." Better Bolshevist battles and the Brave New World than the ancient house of man rotted away silently by such worms of secret sensuality and individual appetite. "The coward does it with a kiss; the brave man with a sword."

But there is, curiously enough, a third thing of the kind, which I am really inclined to think that I dislike even more than the other two. It is not the Communist attacking the family or the Capitalist betraying the family; it is the vast and very astonishing vision of the Hitlerite defending the family. Hitler's way of defending the independence of the family is to make every family dependent on him and his semi-Socialist State; and to preserve the authority of parents by authoritatively telling all the parents what to do. His notion of keeping sacred the dignity of domestic life is to issue peremptory orders that the grandfather is to get up at five in the morning and do dumb-bell exercises, or the grandmother to march twenty miles to a camp to procure a Swastika flag. In other words, he appears to interfere with family life more even than the Bolshevists do; and to do it in the name of the sacredness of the family. It is not much more encouraging than the other two social manifestations; but at least it is more entertaining.

Social Reform vs. Birth Control[*]

Birth Control has an exceedingly unpleasant origin. It is purely capitalist and reactionary. But there are many other aspects of this evil thing. It is unclean in the light of the instincts; it is unnatural in relation to the affections; it is part of a general attempt to run the populace on a routine of quack medicine and smelly science; it is mixed up with a muddled idea that women are free when they serve their employers but slaves when they help their husbands; it is ignorant of the very existence of real households where prudence comes by free-will and agreement....

The very name of "Birth Control" is a piece of pure humbug. It is one of those blatant euphemisms.... It is meant to mean nothing, that it may mean anything, and especially something totally different from what it says. Everybody believes in birth control, and nearly everybody

[*] Excerpt is from "Social Reform vs. Birth Control", in pamphlet, 1927.

has exercised some control over the conditions of birth. People do not get married as somnambulists or have children in their sleep. But throughout numberless ages and nations, the normal and real birth control is called self control. If anybody says it cannot is possibly work, I say it does. In many classes, in many countries where these quack nostrums are unknown, populations of free men have remained within reasonable limits by sound traditions of thrift and responsibility. In so far as there is a local evil of excess, it comes with all other evils from the squalor and despair of our decaying industrialism. But the thing the capitalist newspapers call birth control is not control at all. It is the idea that people should be, in one respect, completely and utterly uncontrolled, so long as they can evade everything in the function that is positive and creative, and intelligent and worthy of a free man. It is a name given to a succession of different expedients, (the one that was used last is always described as having been dreadfully dangerous) by which it is possible to filch the pleasure belonging to a natural process while violently and unnaturally thwarting the process itself.

The nearest and most respectable parallel would be that of the Roman epicure, who took emetics at intervals all day so that he might eat five or six luxurious dinners daily. Now any man's common sense, unclouded by newspaper science and long words, will tell him at once that an operation like that of the epicures is likely in the long run even to be bad for his digestion and pretty certain to be bad for his character. Men left to themselves have sense enough to know when a habit obviously savours of perversion and peril. And if it were the fashion in fashionable circles to call the Roman expedient by the name of "Diet Control " and to talk about it in a lofty fashion as merely "the improvement of life and the service of life" (as if it meant no more than the mastery of man over his meals), we should take the liberty of calling it cant and saying that it had no relation to the reality in debate.

The fact is, I think, that I am in revolt against the conditions of industrial capitalism and the advocates of Birth Control are in revolt against the conditions of human life.... I doubt whether mothers could escape from motherhood into Socialism. But the advocates of Birth Control seem to want some of them to escape from it into capitalism. They seem to express a sympathy with those who prefer "the right to earn outside the home" or (in other words) the right to be a wage-slave and work under the orders of a total stranger because he happens to be a richer man. By what conceivable contortions of twisted thought this ever came to be considered a freer condition than that of companionship with the man she has herself freely accepted, I never could for the life of me make out. The only sense I can make of it is that the proletarian work, though obviously more servile and subordinate than the parental, is so far safer and more irresponsible because it is not parental. I can easily believe that there are some people who do prefer working in a factory to working in a family; for there are always some people who prefer slavery to freedom. But I think their quarrel with motherhood is not like mine, a quarrel with inhuman conditions, but simply a quarrel with life....

Babies and Distributism[*]

I hope it is not a secret arrogance to say that I do not think I am exceptionally arrogant; or if I were, my religion would

---

[*] "Babies and Distributism", in *The Well and the Shallows*, in *CW* 3:439–41.

prevent me from being proud of my pride. Nevertheless, for those of such a philosophy, there is a very terrible
temptation to intellectual pride, in the welter of wordy and
worthless philosophies that surround us today. Yet there are
not many things that move me to anything like a personal
contempt. I do not feel any contempt for an atheist, who
is often a man limited and constrained by his own logic to
a very sad simplification. I do not feel any contempt for a
Bolshevist, who is a man driven to the same negative simplification by a revolt against very positive wrongs. But
there is one type of person for whom I feel what I can only
call contempt. And that is the popular propagandist of what
he or she absurdly describes as Birth-Control.

I despise Birth-Control first because it is a weak and
wobbly and cowardly word. It is also an entirely meaningless word; and is used so as to curry favour even with those
who would at first recoil from its real meaning. The pro-
ceeding these quack doctors recommend does not *control*
any birth. It only makes sure that there shall never be any
birth to control. It cannot, for instance, determine sex, or
even make any selection in the style of the pseudo-science
of Eugenics. Normal people can only act so as to produce
birth; and these people can only act so as to prevent birth.
But these people know perfectly well that they dare not
write the plain word Birth-Prevention, in any one of the
hundred places where they write the hypocritical word
Birth-Control. They know as well as I do that the very
word Birth-Prevention would strike a chill into the public, the instant it was blazoned on headlines, or proclaimed
on platforms, or scattered in advertisements like any other
quack medicine. They dare not call it by its name, because
its name is very bad advertising. Therefore they use a conventional and unmeaning word, which may make the
quack medicine sound more innocuous.

Second, I despise Birth-Control because it is a weak and wobbly and cowardly thing. It is not even a step along the muddy road they call Eugenics; it is a flat refusal to take the first and most obvious step along the road of Eugenics. Once grant that their philosophy is right, and their course of action is obvious; and they dare not take it; they dare not even declare it. If there is no authority in things which Christendom has called moral, because their origins were mystical, then they are clearly free to ignore all difference between animals and men; and treat men as we treat animals. They need not palter with the stale and timid compromise and convention called Birth-Control. Nobody applies it to the cat. The obvious course for Eugenists is to act towards babies as they act towards kittens. Let all the babies be born; and then let us drown those we do not like. I cannot see any objection to it; except the moral or mystical sort of objection that we advance against Birth-Prevention. And that would be real and even reasonable Eugenics; for we could then select the best, or at least the healthiest, and sacrifice what are called the unfit. By the weak compromise of Birth-Prevention, we are very probably sacrificing the fit and only producing the unfit. The births we prevent may be the births of the best and most beautiful children; those we allow, the weakest or worst. Indeed, it is probable; for the habit discourages the early parentage of young and vigorous people; and lets them put off the experience to later years, mostly from mercenary motives. Until I see a real pioneer and progressive leader coming out with a good, bold, scientific programme for drowning babies, I will not join the movement.

But there is a third reason for my contempt, much deeper and therefore much more difficult to express; in which is rooted all my reasons for being anything I am or attempt to be; and above all, for being a Distributist.

Perhaps the nearest to a description of it is to say this: that my contempt boils over into bad behaviour when I hear the common suggestion that a birth is avoided because people want to be "free" to go to the cinema or buy a gramophone or a loudspeaker. What makes me want to walk over such people like doormats is that they use the word "free." By every act of that sort they chain themselves to the most servile and mechanical system yet tolerated by men. The cinema is a machine for unrolling certain regular patterns called pictures; expressing the most vulgar millionaires' notion of the taste of the most vulgar millions. The gramophone is a machine for recording such tunes as certain shops and other organisations choose to sell. The wireless is better; but even that is marked by the modern mark of all three; the impotence of the receptive party. The amateur cannot challenge the actor; the householder will find it vain to go and shout into the gramophone; the mob cannot pelt the modern speaker, especially when he is a loud-speaker. It is all a central mechanism giving out to men exactly what their masters think they should have.

Now a child is the very sign and sacrament of personal freedom. He is a fresh free will added to the wills of the world; he is something that his parents have freely chosen to produce and which they freely agree to protect. They can feel that any amusement he gives (which is often considerable) really comes from him and from them, and from nobody else. He has been born without the intervention of any master or lord. He is a creation and a contribution; he is their own creative contribution to creation. He is also a much more beautiful, wonderful, amusing and astonishing thing than any of the stale stories or jingling jazz tunes turned out by the machines. When men no longer feel that he is so, they have lost the appreciation of primary things, and therefore all sense of proportion about the world. People who prefer the mechanical pleasures, to such a miracle, are jaded and enslaved. They are preferring the very dregs of life to the first fountains of life. They are preferring the last, crooked, indirect, borrowed repeated and exhausted things of our dying Capitalist civilisation, to the reality which is the only rejuvenation of all civilisation. It is they who are hugging the chains of their old slavery; it is the child who is ready for the new world.

Birth and Brain Control[*]

A Correspondent has written to us last week complaining of the article ... which condemned Birth Control not from a religious but a purely rationalist standpoint. The correspondent, Mr. Victor Neuburg, appears to give himself considerable airs of superiority because he is unable to believe in anything and this is interesting, as illustrating a not uncommon combination of the incapacity for believing with the incapacity for thinking. It will be quite sufficient to quote about four lines of his letter, which contain more complicated contradictions and inconsequences than we have ever seen in such a space; and which end with one of those abrupt abysses of the entire absence of humour which is more laughable than the best humour in the world. He says that a man does not practise Birth Control "in order to indulge his passions ... but in order that his quite natural (and therefore legitimate) sexual passion may have no unforeseen and undesired results." Why he should repudiate the indulging of his passion if his passion is quite legitimate, and why he should want to make the indulgence safe except in order to indulge it, the Lord

---

[*] Excerpt was originally published in *G. K.'s Weekly*, July 2, 1927.

only knows. He will pardon this theological expression; which we apologise for not putting in quotation marks, as he so haughtily presents all theological expressions. But the muddle is much more amusing than that. The passion, let it be noted, is not natural and legitimate; he distinctly says it is natural and therefore legitimate. In other words everything that is natural is legitimate. So far so good. It is natural for a man to wish to rush out of a burning theatre, even if he tramples on women and children; it is natural and therefore it is legitimate. It is natural for a man called upon to face death or tortures for the truth to run away and hide; it is natural and therefore it is legitimate. That is quite understood; and so far we are all getting along nicely. But if everything that is natural is right, why in the world is not the birth of a baby as natural as the growth of a passion? If it is unnatural to control appetite, why is it not unnatural to control birth? They are both obviously parts of the same natural process, which has a natural beginning and a natural end. And Mr. Neuburg, who thinks all natural things legitimate, has no possible reason for interrupting it at one stage more than at another. As Nature is infallible, we must not question what progeny she produces. If Nature is not infallible, we have a right to question the passions that she inspires. And then comes the joyous culmination and collapse; of calling a baby an unforeseen consequence of getting married. It would be entertaining to wander through the world with Mr. Neuburg, sharing all the unforeseen consequences of the most ordinary actions. Life must be full of surprises for him; he strikes a match and is indignant that it burns the sulphur; he throws a stone into a puddle and is irritated that it makes a splash; he keeps bees and is furious because they fertilise flowers; he breeds dogs and stands astounded before the unforeseen consequence of puppies. Wonder is a wonderful thing and, with less irritation, might be a beautiful thing. But we rather doubt whether anyone who argues like this has any right to a tone of such extreme intellectual arrogance.

Blasphemy and the Baby*

It was not till Victorian times that the conception of Nature, as the non-human order of things, was turned into a sort of impersonal person. The Victorian agnostic insisted sternly that it must be called She, and must on no account be called He. But to apply this to the Catholic and the other older philosophies is to make a historical mistake about the use of words. When Aristotle said that man is by nature a political animal, he was not thinking of the nineteenth century nightmare about Nature red in tooth and claw. When Catholics talk, as they have always talked, about the natural law, they mean something which could be better translated into modern English as the human law. They mean the law of man's moral status, as it can be perceived by man's natural reason, even without supernatural aid. And when they say that contraception is unnatural, they mean it as they mean that sexual perversion is unnatural. That is, it is unnatural in man, and not merely unnatural in nature. It is something which his own instincts, conscience and imaginative foresight tell him is unworthy of his human dignity; not merely something that interferes with what comes from outside, like a shower of rain or a thunderbolt.

There is no space here to do justice to our very vivid sense of this moral fact; so I will content myself for the moment with a parallel, which has always struck me as

*Excerpt was originally published in *G. K.'s Weekly*, September 27, 1930.

very exact, except that the subject is less serious. If an epicure decided that he could lunch at the Ritz six times a day, and sup at the Savoy seven times in the same evening, by the simple operation of taking emetics between meals, I should have a very strong conviction that he was following an unwholesome course of life. I should think that unlimited gluttony, even when not followed by digestion (or indigestion) would probably in the long run be bad for his body, and would quite certainly be bad for his mind. I think the same of unlimited lust without its natural consequences. I think it would have other and much less natural consequences.

One proof of its unnatural character is that the theory starts everybody on an unnatural way of thinking; even Mr. A. P. Herbert. For instance, I feel it to be utterly unnatural, though it is already quite stale and conventional, to talk in this queer contemptuous way about the birth of a child. Mr. Herbert breaks out into a sort of romantic, not to say sentimental, indignation against the remark that the chief object of marriage is the procreation of children. He calls it all sorts of funny things which are supposed to be withering; such as masculine and mediaeval and smacking of the stud farm; an odd thing to associate with what is mediaeval, since the eugenic fancy is peculiarly modern. Well, Catholics will not resent being called masculine and are used to being called mediaeval. But what strikes me as truly extraordinary is the implication that there is something low about the objective being the birth of a child. Whereas it is obvious that this great natural miracle is the one creative, imaginative and disinterested part of the whole business. The creation of a new creature, not ourselves, of a new conscious center, of a new and independent focus of experience and enjoyment, is an immeasurably more grand and godlike act even than a real love affair; how much more superior to a momentary physical satisfaction. If creating another self is not noble, why is pure self-indulgence nobler?

Scipio and the Children*

I have lately found myself in the town of Tarragona; famous for its vinegar, which it wisely sends abroad, rather than the wine, which it still more wisely drinks at home. I have myself ordered a fair amount of the wine; I omitted to order any of the vinegar. The thing that struck me first and last in Spain was the Spanish children; especially the Spanish little boys, and their relation to the Spanish fathers. The love of fathers and sons in this country is one of the great poems of Christendom; it has, like a bewildering jewel, a hundred beautiful aspects, and especially that supremely beautiful aspect; that it is a knock in the eye for that nasty-minded old pedant Freud.

I was sitting at a cafe table with another English traveller, and I was looking at a little boy with a bow and arrows, who discharged very random shafts in all directions, and periodically turned in triumph and flung himself into the arms of his father, who was a waiter. That part of the scene was repeated all over the place, with fathers of every social type and trade. And it is no good to tell me that such humanities must be peculiar to this Catalan town. And it is no good to tell me that Spaniards are all gloomy and harsh and cruel, for I have seen the children; I have also seen the parents. I may also remark that one element winch specially haunts me, in the Spanish Peninsula, is the very elusive element called Liberty. Nobody seems to have the itch of interference; nobody is moved by that great motto of so much social legislation; "Go and

* Excerpt was originally published in *G. K.'s Weekly*, May 30, 1935.

see what Tommy is doing, and tell him he mustn't." Considering what this Tommy was doing, I am fairly sure that in most progressive countries, somebody would tell him he mustn't. He shot an arrow that hit his father; probably because he was aiming at something else. He shot an arrow that hit me; but I am a BROAD target. His bow and his archery were quite inadequate; and would not have been tolerated in the scientific Archery School into which he would no doubt have been instantly drafted in any state in which sport is taken as seriously as it should be. While I was staring at him, the English traveller interrupted my dream by saying suddenly:

"What is there to *see* in Tarragona?"

I was instantly prompted to answer, and almost did answer, "Why, of course, the boy with the bow and arrows! There is also the waiter."

But I stopped myself in time, remembering the strange philosophy of sightseeing; and then I found my mind rather a blank. I knew next to nothing about the town, and said so. I said the Cathedral was very fine; and then added with increasing vagueness; "I'm afraid I don't know anything at all about Tarragona. I have a hazy idea that Scipio got buried here or born here. I can't even remember which."

"Who?" he inquired patiently.

"Scipio," I said, with an increasing sense of weakness; then I added as in feeble self-defence, "Africanus."

He inquired whether I meant that the man was an African. I said that I was sure he was not an African; I believed he was a Roman; certainly he was a Roman General; and I thought it was too early in history for a Roman General to have really belonged to what were afterwards the Roman Provinces. I had always understood that Carthage, or the Carthaginian influence, practically prevailed over all these parts at that time. And even as I said the words a thought came to me, like a blinding and even a blasting light.

The traveller was very legitimately bored. After the mysterious manner of his kind, he was not bored with sightseeing, but he was bored with history; especially ancient history. I do not blame him for that; I only puzzle upon why a man bored with history should take endless trouble to visit historic sites. He was patently one of those who think that all those things happened such a long time ago that they cannot make much difference now. But it had suddenly occurred to me that this rather remote example really might, perhaps, make a great deal of difference now. I tried to tell him so; and he must have formed the impression that I was raving mad.

"Would it be all the same," I asked, "if that little boy were thrown into a furnace as a religious ceremony, when his family went to church on Sunday? That is what Carthage did; it worshipped Moloch; and sacrificed batches of babies as a regular religious ritual.

"That is what Scipo Africanus did; he defeated Carthage, when it had nearly defeated the world. Somehow, I seem to feel a fine shade of difference."

My companion did not reply; and I continued to watch the archer; and though Apollo was a Pagan god, I am glad that such a sun-god slew the Punic Python; and that even before the Faith, those ancient arrows cast down Moloch for us all.

The Large Family[*]

The ... Large Family ... is a point about which most modern writers tell nothing but lies. It was not a very large family by the older standards; but it represents the atmosphere of the large family as compared with conditions very

[*] Excerpt was originally published in *G. K.'s Weekly*, July 12, 1934.

common to-day. It is intensely typical that modern educationists and psychologists never talk about children. They talk about The Child. The very phrase suggests the concentrated spotlights, searchlights, electric torches, microscopes and magnifying-glasses all turned inwards upon one wretched child; the heir of all the ages and possibly the last of the human race. As between the two pictures of half-a-dozen adults studying one child and half-a-dozen children tormenting one adult, I have no doubt at all that the children were happier than the child. But there were advantages in real psychology. Moderns talk most horrible nonsense about the needs of The Child, whether in toys or tests. As if it were not more fun to have living toys to play with.

5

Parents ... and Public Education

Grass and children
There seems no end to them.
But if there were but one blade of grass
Men would see that it is fairer than lilies,
And if we saw the first child
We should worship it as the God come on earth.

* * *

I would say to all parents
Do you take things equally
How do you know that you are not
In the place of Joseph and Mary.

You and I would certainly not be the splendid public monuments that we are if our fathers and mothers had not given us not only a great deal more devotion than we deserved, but a great deal more devotion than we in any strictly ascertainable and scientific sense required. But that immoderate consideration was necessary to produce even moderate results; the infant has to be treated as much better than he is so that in the long run he may be not quite so bad as he might have been. The child has to begin as a god, in the faint hope that he may end as a man.

—*Daily News*, June 24, 1905

If you really wish to bend yourself to the heroic and saintly task of reconciling two men—Robinson and Brown—who had a genuine and bitter quarrel, it would be well to begin with the fact that each man has a family, and that even his public irregularities are sometimes directed by his private affections. The only palliation of the pettifogging pedantry which is so regrettable in Robinson is to be found in the unconscious faces of the nine little Robinsons. The only excuse for the gambling recklessness which we all lament in Mr. Brown is the persuasive charm which we all recognise in Mrs. Brown. These are the things which might conceivably and truly make men forgive their enemies. We can only turn hate to love by understanding what are the things that men have loved.... [They] are most likely to be reconciled when they remember for a moment that they are two fathers.

—*Illustrated London News*, June 4, 1921

The books that should be set before children are books of play and ceremonial, and pomp and war: the whole *gloria mundi*, the whole pageant of history, full of blood and pride, may safely be told them—everything but the secret of their own incomparable influence. Children need to be taught primarily the grandeur of the whole world. It is merely the whole world that needs to be taught the grandeur of children.

—*The Speaker*, November 24, 1900

A surprise, in the sublime and philosophical sense in which the word is used by children in the nursery, really is perhaps the highest happiness allowed to humanity. It is glorious to get something we do want and do not expect. But in many of the "wonders" which science now predicts, it is really rather the other way. It is not something that we do want and do not expect. It is much more often something we don't want and do expect. Or, if we want it, we want it only as the completion of a system of scientific conveniences which we have long expected to see completed. What is called Television is an excellent example of this. We emphatically do expect it, even if we never get it. We expect it because it is the completion or the combination of two things with which we are already familiar; one might almost say, with which we are already bored.

— *G.K.'s Weekly*, May 21, 1927

We are perpetually told that the world must be surrendered to the young. But ... the real complaint is not so much that the young are young as that the young are old.... It is the complaint that boys and girls have grown up too quickly; not that they have remained children too long.

— *G. K.'s Weekly*, July 21, 1928

Men like Mr. H.G. Wells are perpetually talking about posterity, and our duty of looking to the next generation, and living for the next generation. And all the time he continues to look very coldly on the only institution in which people really do to a great extent live for and in their children; the respectable Christian family.

—*G. K.'s Weekly*, October 13, 1928

The progressive child of the twentieth century, with his earphones or his loud speaker.... When he puts the earphones to his ears he does in fact put a mouth-gag into his mouth; as compared with the normal conversationalist conducting normal conversations. There is no harm in it, of course, in its proper place and proportion. But to fill your house, and fill your head, with voices you cannot answer, with cries you cannot return, with arguments you cannot dispute, with sentiments you cannot either applaud or denounce, is to enter into a one-sided relation and to live a lopsided life. The five senses used to be called the five wits; and to depend wholly on the receptive side of them is to be in a real sense half-witted.

— G.K.'s Weekly, May 3, 1930

The modern novel has gone through a series of stages, of which the first might be stamped with the general motto of "Boys will be Boys." Then came the earnest late Victorian novel of emancipation and the ethics of sex; which might bear the motto "Girls will be Boys." And finally, we are left with the very latest psychological and neurotic sort of novel, which seems to carry the cognizance of "Boys won't be Boys."

— G. K.'s Weekly, July 12, 1934

What is information? What is good information? What are the things of and with which a living man should be informed? The first things, one would fancy, would be the roots of his own life; where his bread comes from, and how it can practically be produced out of the earth; where his family comes from, and what are the traditions of his home and the true witness of his fathers to the facts of history. That is the sort of education which ... our modern instruction utterly destroys and sweeps away.

— G.K.'s Weekly, August 30, 1930

A magistrate recently remarked ... that this new lawlessness was due to the loss of parental control. And I think it reasonable, whether the magistrate thought so or not, to say that the loss of parental control is in its turn due to the increase of official control. And this is surely the more natural because it is an increase of official control over parents.... This is especially true to the eclipse of the father by the schoolmaster.

— New Witness, October 21, 1921

The [school]master must at best teach morality mainly in
theory; while the mother is obliged to teach it in practice.

— *New Witness*, October 21, 1921

The truth is that all our educational experiments are in the
wrong direction. They are concerned with turning children, not only into men, but into modern men; whereas
modern men need nothing so much as to be made a little
more like children. The whole object of real education is
a renascence of wonder, a revival of that receptiveness to
which poetry and religion appeal.

— *New Witness*, October 28, 1921

Of course, it would be worth while to pay a big price
to get a well-informed people. At the present moment
we are paying an abominably big price to get a more and
more ill-informed people.

— *G. K.'s Weekly*, August 30, 1930

Nobody can take in the scale of the modern changes, let
alone feel free enough of them to note what is sinister or
dubious about them. For instance, nobody has yet measured the meaning of State education, with its practical
elimination of the parent.

— *Illustrated London News*, July 9, 1932

It seems to me that since the science of economics appeared, the world has committed two enormous acts of
waste. The first was throwing away a supernatural power,
and the second a natural power. The first was destroying the monastic impulse and the second the parental
impulse. There were certain queer people who were
ready to help men without payment, for the love of God.
There were, what is still more extraordinary, people who
were prepared to look after us in our hideous infancy for

the love of us. Modern economy and efficiency consist in
paying other people to do what these people would do
for nothing.

— *G. K.'s Weekly*, September 4, 1926

If children see that their teachers despise what their parents
desire, there is and must be a conflict of authorities. And
there is, and must be, in the modern State, a monstrous
discovery; that it is the more new and unnatural authority
that has the power.

— *New Witness*, December 27, 1918

It is especially awkward, when the young man who has
never learned anything except how to hate his own father
and grandfather, is suddenly called upon to love all men
like brothers.

— "About Modern Girls", *As I Was Saying*

Turning Inside Out[*]

When the author of *If Winter Comes*[1] brought out another
book about the life of the family, it was almost as much
criticized as the first book was praised. I do not say that
there was nothing to criticize, but I do say that I was not
convinced by the abstract logic of the criticism. Probably the critics would have accepted it as a true story if
the author had not been so incautious as to give it a true
moral. And the moral is not fashionable in the press at the
moment; for it is to the effect that a woman may gain a

[*] "Turning Inside Out", in *Fancies vs. Fads* (London: Methuen, 1923), pp.
193–204.
[1] *If Winter Comes* is a best-selling novel about divorce by A. S. M. Hutchinson.

professional success at the price of a domestic failure. And
it is the convention of journalism at this moment to support what is feminist against what is feminine. Anyhow,
while the story might be criticized, the criticisms can certainly be criticized. It is not really conclusive to say that a
woman may be ambitious in business without her children
going to the bad. It is just as easy to say that a woman
may be ambitious in politics without helping to murder an
old gentleman in his bed. But that does not make *Macbeth*
either inartistic or untrue. It is just as easy to say that a
woman may be ambitious in society without tricking her
husband into a debtor's prison, so that she may spend the
time with a bald-headed nobleman with red whiskers. But
that does not make the great scene in *Vanity Fair* uncon-
vincing either in detail or design. The question in fiction
is not whether that thing must occur, but whether that sort
of thing may occur, and whether it is significant of larger
things. Now this business of the woman at work and the
woman at home is a very large thing, and this story about
it is highly significant.

For in this matter the modern mind is inconsistent with
itself. It has managed to get one of its rather crude ideals
in flat contradiction to the other. People of the progressive sort are perpetually telling us that the hope of the
world is in education. Education is everything. Nothing
is so important as training the rising generation. Nothing is really important except the rising generation. They
tell us this over and over again, with slight variations of
the same formula, and never seem to see what it involves.
For if there be any word of truth in all this talk about the
education of the child, then there is certainly nothing but
nonsense in nine-tenths of the talk about the emancipation of the woman. If education is the highest function in
the State, why should anybody want to be emancipated

from the highest function in the State? It is as if we talked of commuting the sentence that condemned a man to be President of the United States; or a reprieve coming in time to save him from being Pope. If education is the largest thing in the world, what is the sense of talking about a woman being liberated from the largest thing in the world? It is as if we were to rescue her from the cruel doom of being a poet like Shakespeare; or to pity the limitations of an all-round artist like Leonardo da Vinci. Nor can there be any doubt that there is truth in this claim for education. Only precisely the sort of which it is particularly true is the sort called domestic education. Private education really is universal. Public education can be comparatively narrow. It would really be an exaggeration to say that the schoolmaster who takes his pupils in freehand drawing is training them in all the uses of freedom. It really would be fantastic to say that the harmless foreigner who instructs a class in French or German is talking with all the tongues of men and angels. But the mother dealing with her own daughters in her own home does literally have to deal with all forms of freedom, because she has to deal with all sides of a single human soul. She is obliged, if not to talk with the tongues of men and angels, at least to decide how much she shall talk about angels and how much about men.

In short, if education is really the larger matter, then certainly domestic life is the larger matter; and official or commercial life the lesser matter. It is a mere matter of arithmetic that anything taken from the larger matter will leave it less. It is a mere matter of simple subtraction that the mother must have less time for the family if she has more time for the factory. If education, ethical and cultural, really were a trivial and mechanical matter, the mother might possibly rattle through it as a rapid routine, before going about her more serious business of serving a capitalist for hire. If education were merely instruction, she might briefly instruct her babies in the multiplication tables, before she mounted to higher and nobler spheres as the servant of a Milk Trust or the secretary of a Drug Combine. But the moderns are perpetually assuring us that education is not instruction; they are perpetually insisting that it is not a mechanical exercise, and must on no account be an abbreviated exercise. It must go on at every hour. It must cover every subject. But if it must go on at all hours, it must not be neglected in business hours. And if the child is to be free to cover every subject, the parent must be free to cover every subject too.

For the idea of a non-parental substitute is simply an illusion of wealth. The advanced advocate of this inconsistent and infinite education for the child is generally thinking of the rich child; and all this particular sort of liberty should rather be called luxury. It is natural enough for a fashionable lady to leave her little daughter with the French governess or the Czecho-Slovakian governess or the Ancient Sanskrit governess, and know that one or other of these sides of the infant's intelligence is being developed; while she, the mother, figures in public as a money-lender or some other modern position of dignity. But among poorer people there cannot be five teachers to one pupil. Generally there are about fifty pupils to one teacher. There it is impossible to cut up the soul of a single child and distribute it among specialists. It is all we can do to tear in pieces the soul of a single schoolmaster, and distribute it in rags and scraps to a whole mob of boys. And even in the case of the wealthy child it is by no means clear that specialists are a substitute for spiritual authority. Even a millionaire can never be certain that he has not left out one governess, in the long procession of governesses perpetually passing under his marble portico;

and the omission may be as fatal as that of the king who forgot to ask the bad fairy to the christening. The daughter, after a life of ruin and despair, may look back and say, "Had I but also had a Lithuanian governess, my fate as a diplomatist's wife in Eastern Europe would have been very different." But it seems rather more probable, on the whole, that what she would miss would not be one or other of these special accomplishments, but some commonsense code of morals or general view of life. The millionaire could, no doubt, hire a mahatma or mystical prophet to give his child a general philosophy. But I doubt if the philosophy would be very successful even for the rich child, and it would be quite impossible for the poor child. In the case of comparative poverty, which is the common lot of mankind, we come back to a general parental responsibility, which is the common sense of mankind. We come back to the parent as the person in charge of education. If you exalt the education, you must exalt the parental power with it. If you exaggerate the education, you must exaggerate the parental power with it. If you depreciate the parental power, you most depreciate education with it. If the young are always right and can do as they like, well and good; let us all be jolly, old and young, and free from every kind of responsibility. But in that case do not come pestering us with the importance of education, when nobody has any authority to educate anybody. Make up your mind whether you want unlimited education or unlimited emancipation, but do not be such a fool as to suppose you can have both at once.

There is evidence, as I have noted, that the more hard-headed people, even of the most progressive sort, are beginning to come back to realities in this respect. People are no longer quite so certain that a woman's liberty consists of having a latch-key without a house. They are no longer wholly convinced that every housekeeper is dull and prosaic, while every bookkeeper is wild and poetical. And among the intelligent the reaction is actually strengthened by all the most modern excitements about psychology and hygiene. We cannot insist that every trick of nerves or train of thought is important enough to be searched for in libraries and laboratories, and not important enough for anybody to watch by simply staying at home. We cannot insist that the first years of infancy are of supreme importance, and that mothers are not of supreme importance; or that motherhood is a topic of sufficient interest for men, but not of sufficient interest for mothers. Every word that is said about the tremendous importance of trivial nursery habits goes to prove that being a nurse is not trivial. All tends to the return of the simple truth that the private work is the great one and the public work the small. The human house is a paradox, for it is larger inside than out.

But in the problem of private versus public life there is another neglected truth. It is true of many masculine problems as well as of this feminine problem. Indeed, feminism falls here into exactly the same mistake as militarism and imperialism. I mean that anything on a grand scale gives the illusion of a grand success. Curiously enough, multiplication acts as a concealment. Repetition actually disguises failure. Take a particular man, and tell him to put on a particular kind of hat and coat and trousers, and to stand in particular attitudes in the back garden; and you will have great difficulty in persuading yourself (or him) that he has passed through a triumph and transfiguration. Order four hundred such hats, and eight hundred such trousers, and you will have turned the fancy costume into a uniform. Make all the four hundred men stand in the special attitudes on Salisbury Plain, and there will rise up before you the spirit of a regiment. Let the regiment march past, and, if you have any life in you above the brutes that perish, you will have an overwhelming sense that something splendid has just happened, or is just going to begin. I sympathize with this moral emotion in militarism; I think it does symbolize something great in the soul, which has given us the image of St. Michael. But I also realize that in practical relations that emotion can get mixed up with an illusion. It is not really possible to know the characters of all the four hundred men in the marching column as well as one might know the character of the one man attitudinizing in the back garden. If all the four hundred men were individual failures, we could still vaguely feel that the whole thing was a success. If we know the one man to be a failure, we cannot think him a success.

That is why a footman has become rather a foolish figure, while a foot-soldier remains rather a sublime one. Or rather, that is one of the reasons; for there are others much more worthy. Anyhow, footmen were only formidable or dignified when they could come in large numbers like foot-soldiers—when they were in fact the feudal army of some great local family, having some of the loyalty of local patriotism. Then a livery was as dignified as a uniform, because it really was a uniform. A man who said he served the Nevilles or rode with the Douglases could once feel much like a man fighting for France or England. But military feeling is mob feeling, noble as mob feeling may be. Parading one footman is like lunching on one pea, or curing baldness by the growth of one hair. There ought not to be anything but a plural for flunkeys, any more than for measles or vermin or animalculae or the sweets called hundreds and thousands. Strictly speaking, I suppose that a logical Latinist could say, "I have seen an animalcula"; but

I never heard of a child having the moderation to remark, "I have eaten a hundred and thousand." Similarly, any one of us can feel that to have hundreds and thousands of slaves, let alone soldiers, might give a certain imaginative pleasure in magnificence. To have one slave reveals all the meanness of slavery. For the solitary flunkey really is the man in fancy dress, the man standing in the back-garden in the strange and the fantastic coat and breeches. His isolation reveals our illusion. We find our failure in the back-garden, when we have been dreaming a dream of success in the market-place. When you ride through the streets amid a great mob of vassals (you may have noticed) you have a genial and not ungenerous sense of being at one with them all. You cannot remember their names or count their numbers, but their very immensity seems a substitute for intimacy. That is what great men have felt at the head of great armies; and the reason why Napoleon or Foch would call his soldiers "*mes enfants.*" He feels at that moment that they are a part of him, as if he had a million arms and legs. But it is very different if you disband your army of lackeys; or if (as is, after all, possible) you have not got an army of lackeys. It is very different if you look at one lackey; one solitary solemn footman standing in your front hall. You never have the sense of being caught up into a rapture of unity with *him.* All your sense of social solidarity with your social inferiors has dropped from you. It is only in public that people can be so intimate as that. When you look into the eyes of the lonely footman, you see that his soul is far away.

In other words, you find yourself at the foot of a steep and staggering mountain crag, that is the real character and conscience of a man. To be really at one with that man, you would have to solve real problems and believe that your own solutions were real. In dealing with the one man you would really have a far huger and harder job than in dealing with your throng of thousands. And *that* is the job that people run away from when they wish to escape from domesticity to public work, especially educational work. They wish to escape from a sense of failure which is simply a sense of fact. They wish to recapture the illusion of the market-place. It is an illusion that departs in the dark interiors of domesticity, where the realities dwell. As I have said, I am very far from condemning it altogether; it is a lawful pleasure, and a part of life, in its proper proportion, like any other. But I am concerned to point out to the feminists and the faddists that it is not an approach to truth, but rather the opposite. Publicity is rather of the nature of a harmless romance. Public life at its very best will contain a great deal of harmless romancing, and much more often of very harmful romancing. In other words, I am concerned with pointing out that the passage from private life to public life, while it may be right or wrong, or necessary or unnecessary, or desirable or undesirable, is always of necessity a passage from a greater work to a smaller one, and from a harder work to an easier one. And that is why most of the moderns do wish to pass from the great domestic task to the smaller and easier commercial one. They would rather provide the liveries of a hundred footmen than be bothered with the love-affairs of one. They would rather take the salutes of a hundred soldiers than try to save the soul of one. They would rather serve out income-tax papers or telegraph forms to a hundred men than meals, conversation, and moral support to one. They would rather arrange the educational course in history or geography, or correct the examination papers in algebra or trigonometry, for a hundred children, than struggle with the whole human character of one. For anyone who makes himself responsible for one small baby, as a whole, will soon find that he is wrestling with gigantic angels and demons.

In another way there is something of illusion, or of irresponsibility, about the purely public function, especially in the case of public education. The educationist generally deals with only one section of the pupil's mind. But he always deals with only one section of the pupil's life. The parent has to deal, not only with the whole of the child's character, but also with the whole of the child's career. The teacher sows the seed, but the parent reaps as well as sows. The schoolmaster sees more children, but it is not clear that he sees more childhood; certainly he sees less youth and no maturity. The number of little girls who take prussic acid is necessarily small. The boys who hang themselves on bed-posts, after a life of crime, are generally the minority. But the parent has to envisage the whole life of the individual, and not merely the school life of the scholar. It is not probable that the parent will exactly anticipate crime and prussic acid as the crown of the infant's career. But he will anticipate hearing of the crime if it is committed; he will probably be told of the suicide if it takes place. It is quite doubtful whether the schoolmaster or schoolmistress will ever hear of it at all. Everybody knows that teachers have a harassing and often heroic task, but it is not unfair to them to remember that in this sense they have an exceptionally happy task. The cynic would say that the teacher is happy in never seeing the results of his own teaching. I prefer to confine myself to saying that he has not the extra worry of having to estimate it from the other end. The teacher is seldom in at the death. To take a milder theatrical metaphor, he is seldom there on the night. But this is only one of many instances of the same truth: that what is called public life is not larger than private life, but smaller. What we call public life is a fragmentary affair of sections and seasons and impressions; it is only in private life that dwells the fullness of our life bodily.

Playgrounds for Adults[*]

In a previous article I ventured to maintain the general position that children were in several matters, of which the institution of play was the strongest example, more human than adults; I had almost said more mature. For, indeed, a great many adults, such as undergraduates and young stockbrokers, do give rein to the institution of play, light bonfires, break windows, wrench off knockers, and celebrate the British Empire. But the play of the adults is really childish; it is blundering, designless, and inconclusive, whilst the play of children is rounded, rhythmic, and intelligible. And from this I venture to deduce that there was an actual gap in the life and culture of the adult, that they had left behind half their human nature as much as if they were monks or lunatics, and if this is so, it is clear that children can along supply the gap. Grown-up people may be in some small degree useful to teach children to work, but children are even more urgently needed to teach grown-up people to play. As it is, we set one adult to teach a room full of babies. In the future, perhaps, we may set one baby to teach, with considerable severity, a room full of adults.

In this article I wish to suggest something of the practical side of the necessity and its relation to the various games which children play. But, first of all, I must point out a distinction the neglect of which may give rise to

---

[*] Excerpt was originally published in *The Speaker*, November 30, 1901.

some confusion. Games as ordinarily understood do not
constitute play, they constitute sport. In a game, as the
adult understands a game, the essential is competition, and
the aim victory. In a game as children understand it the
essential is rather a certain artistic delight in the group-
ing and ceremony of the fictitious characters of the affair.
They do not play for victory, they play, so far as their
aim can be defined, for self-deception. It is a matter of
art for art's sake; they wish to pass into that kind of pictorial trance which we are all seeking when we read books
or listen to music. Perhaps the impulse most resembling
a child's love of play is the impulse which leads us to go
to the theatre. It is significant that the theatre was originally what children's play is, a festival, a strictly ceremonial rejoicing. Children merely reproduce the theatre in
a more human, direct, and powerful manner, by being
themselves both the spectators and the actors. In any case,
in short, we must rid ourselves of the notion that children
take chiefly a competitive or sporting interest in play. One
of the most universal and popular forms of play amongst
children is that represented by "Here we go round the
mulberry-bush," which consists of nothing but running
round in a ring. It consists of the circle, the very type of
equality and communism, the figure in which all points
are equally distant from the centre. Such games as "Here
we go round the mulberry-bush" may be said to constitute
the first class of children's games, the purely ritualistic. In
an age when the sense of ritual is supposed to have been
revived it is nothing short of scandalous that human beings
in the fulness of life and strength have not revived these
elementary and beautiful movements. The aesthetic school
may plaster a whole world with dados and deck it with
peacocks' feathers before they invent anything so beautiful as six children dancing in a ring. These ceremonial

games might be the means of re-introducing that happy ritualism, that hilarious love of order, that passion for rules and observances, which is the mark of children and wise men. The formal games might, in the hands of great artists, become national and decorative dances. The rude rhymes which are sung to them might blossom, as the ancient legends have blossomed, into elevated poetry. Perhaps the unfortunate adult intellect would be more reconciled to them if this were so....

High above the[se games], and at the head of another class, towers the great and Royal game of "Hide and Seek," the noblest of all earthly games, and the game that includes all others. How the majority of men and women in this world can waste their time in childish amusement, such as golf and rabbit-shooting, while reflecting pastime of the gods, is indeed one of the riddles of existence. "Hide and Seek" is the greatest of games, because like war, it has the whole earth for its chess-board. Every object of the landscape, tree or hole or hedge, has, like a huge chess-man, its own peculiar powers and functions in the game. A tree may be valuable because it is high, a wall because it is low, a bank because it is slippery, a rock because it is firm. The game includes planning, thinking, remembering, inventing, running, climbing, jumping, seeing, hearing, and waiting. The player has the emotions of all the outlaws since the world began. We may think long and hard before any of us can understand why this great terrestrial warfare, this ancient and earth-born strategy, should be considered childish, knocking little balls about with sticks considered manly. "Hide and Seek" is surely a greater thing than the absurd-shooting of tiny little beasts and birds, which does not, to the really sportsmanlike spirit, differ very much from shooting bluebottles. For "Hide and Seek" is the noblest of all sports and chases, the hunting of man.

The Distributist Schoolmaster[*]

There is an aspect of the Education Controversy which specially concerns Distributists, apart from the way in which it concerns Catholics or Protestants or Agnostics. It is the aspect in which only the State is exalted above the School; and the Family is deprived of all influence over the School, as it has been largely deprived of all influence over the State. According to the simple notions of a more normal time, the State consists of the parents of families and the School consists of the children of families, undergoing special training by persons *in loco parentis*, representing the parents in the School, as the parents represent the families in the State. Quite apart from the negative effect of new systems on religion, there is their positive effect on politics; in that they enormously increase the importance of the State, as distinct even from the citizens of the State.

Modern Thought, so called because it began more than a hundred years ago and has grown more thoughtless ever since, has this special defect among many others: that it does not understand detachment or intellectual independence. It will not face facts, and if any man in a disinterested manner points out a fact, it accuses him generally of uttering a paradox and always of trying to prove a point. Nobody, or nobody in the newspaper world which counts to-day, has noted a fact first pointed out by Mr. Belloc, I think, but, when once pointed out, obvious to any objective and realistic mind. It is that State Compulsory Education is a tremendous thing, potentially a tremendous tyranny, and by its very nature doing very much what all religious persecution attempted to do. If you punish people for not sending their children to schools, where some

[*] Excerpt was originally published in *G. K.'s Weekly*, August 16, 1930.

view of life (however vague) is implanted, you may be
conducting education, and you may be justified in conducting education, but you are conducting persecution.
The logic of the thing has not altered by the fact that light
penalties are attached to those who will not accept the
State teaching, when heavy penalties used to be attached
to those who started some positive opposition teaching.
You are, in fact, using the Secular Arm in the things of the
Spirit; even if you call it the Spirit of Progress or the Spirit
of True Christianity. And, in fact, the power has been used
for things much less spiritual, not for Progress but for Prus-
sianism; not for true Christianity but for tribal heathenism.

A journalistic debate still lingers about What Caused
the Great War. I should say that education caused the
Great War. I should say that those huge combinations
were the result of the compulsory culture peculiar to
modern times. Dean Inge and other critics of Christian
tradition always treat the Catholic school as something
fitted up with all the engines of the Spanish Inquisition.
But that is because they live in the past, in the time of the
Spanish Inquisition, and have not yet heard of the Great
War. Take the facts of modern Europe as they really stood
in still recent times, and the truth is just the other way.
Nobody believes that an ordinary Bavarian, left alone
with his Catholic home and his Catholic school, with his
relaxations of music and Munich beer, would ever have
evolved all by himself the idea that he was a Super-man
or a Nordic War-Lord eugenically destined to conquer
the world. All that theory that Germany was one nation,
that it was a Super-Nation, that it was a chosen people
organically superior to Latins, Slavs and Celts, that never
came out of Munich beer or music; it most certainly
never came out of Catholic schools or Catholic doctrines.
That was imposed entirely, exclusively and forcibly, by

the huge modern machine of universal instruction, which printed and stamped the Prussian idea upon every town from Poznan to Metz. I am not specially raising the question of war-guilt, though I have never changed my view of it; for indeed this particular generalisation was true in a lesser degree of the Allies also. The French State, in a much more civilised way, forced all citizens to learn the patriotism which divided nations, but not the religion that unites them. The English, in a much more genial fashion, were educated in national narrowness, and it was made compulsory to sing "What is the Meaning of Empire Day?" while it would be thought "sectarian" to sing the *Dies Irae* about the common doom of all mankind.

In a word, Compulsory Education is Conscription. It is as modern as Conscription, as scientifically organised as Conscription, and it acted in international affairs in exactly the same manner as Conscription. This does not in itself prove that Compulsory Education is necessarily wrong. I do not myself think that Conscription is necessarily wrong. But what we now call Education does belong to that class of coercive, militant and sometimes servile things represented by the organisation of a modern army rather than by the emancipation or eccentricity of a modern poem. It is a great iron engine for hammering something, generally the same thing, into great masses of merely passive humanity. And anyone who is moved, as we are, to set the man against the machine, will have a certain suspicion of it at the start.

For us the practical inference is this. Long before we can hope to abolish the huge centralised system of culture, even supposing that we really want to abolish it, we can do a great deal by standing out for exceptions, sometimes for exceptions merely because they are exceptional.... That is what the Distributist can do in the case of the

alternative institutions that may balance the autocracy of
State Instruction. He can do it especially, because of his
social convictions, in the case of the poor family. He can
do it, whatever his religious convictions, in the case of
the Catholic School. He is fully justified, merely as a Distributist, in supporting anything that defends the domestic
and individual organisation of mankind; for, whatever he
may think of theocracies and religious despotism in the
past, there has never been so dull or deadly a factory for
the manufacture of minds.

On Dangerous Toys*

It would be too high and hopeful a compliment to say
that the world is becoming absolutely babyish. For its chief
weak-mindedness is an inability to appreciate the intelligence of babies. On every side we hear whispers and
warnings that would have appeared half-witted to the
Wise Men of Gotham. Only this Christmas I was told in
a toy-shop that not so many bows and arrows were being
made for little boys; because they were considered dangerous. It might in some circumstances be dangerous to have
a little bow. It is always dangerous to have a little boy. But
no other society, claiming to be sane, would have dreamed
of supposing that you could abolish all bows unless you
could abolish all boys. With the merits of the latter reform
I will not deal here. There is a great deal to be said for such
a course; and perhaps we shall soon have an opportunity of
considering it. For the modern mind seems quite incapable
of distinguishing between the means and the end, between
the organ and the disease, between the use and the abuse;

* Excerpt was originally published in *Illustrated London News*, January 7, 1922.

and would doubtless break the boy along with the bow, as it empties out the baby with the bath.

But let us, by way of a little study in this mournful state of things, consider this case of the dangerous toy. Now the first and most self-evident truth is that, of all the things a child sees and touches, the most dangerous toy is about the least dangerous thing. There is hardly a single domestic utensil that is not much more dangerous than a little bow and arrows. He can burn himself in the fire, he can boil himself in the bath, he can cut his throat with the carving-knife, he can scald himself with the kettle, he can choke himself with anything small enough, he can break his neck off anything high enough. He moves all day long amid a murderous machinery, as capable of killing and maiming as the wheels of the most frightful factory. He plays all day in a house fitted up with engines of torture like the Spanish Inquisition. And while he thus dances in the shadow of death, he is to be saved from all the perils of possessing a piece of string, tied to a bent bough or twig. When he is a little boy it generally takes him some time even to learn how to hold the bow. When he does hold it, he is delighted if the arrow flutters for a few yards like a feather or an autumn leaf. But even if he grows a little older and more skillful, and has yet not learned to despise arrows in favour of aeroplanes, the amount of damage he could conceivably do with his little arrows would be about one hundredth part of the damage that he could always in any case have done by simply picking up a stone in the garden.

Now you do not keep a little boy from throwing stones by preventing him from ever seeing stones. You do not do it by locking up all the stones in the Geological Museum, and only issuing tickets of admission to adults. You do not do it by trying to pick up all the pebbles on the beach, for fear he should practice throwing them into the sea. You do not even adopt so obvious and even pressing a social reform as forbidding roads to be made of anything but asphalt, or directing that all gardens shall be made on clay and none on gravel. You neglect all these great opportunities opening before you; you neglect all these inspiring vistas of social science and enlightenment. When you want to prevent a child from throwing stones, you fall back on the stalest and most sentimental and even most superstitious methods. You do it by trying to preserve some reasonable authority and influence over the child. You trust to your private relation with the boy, and not to your public relation with the stone. And what is true of the natural missile is just as true, of course, of the artificial missile; especially as it is a very much more ineffectual and therefore innocuous missile. A man could be really killed, like St. Stephen, with the stones in the road. I doubt if he could be really killed, like St. Sebastian, with the arrows in the toyshop. But anyhow the very plain principle is the same. If you can teach a child not to throw a stone, you can teach him when to shoot an arrow; if you cannot teach him anything, he will always have something to throw. If he can be persuaded not to smash the Archdeacon's hat with a heavy flint, it will probably be possible to dissuade him from transfixing that head-dress with a toy arrow. If his training deters him from heaving half a brick at the postman, it will probably also warn him against constantly loosening shafts of death against the policeman. But the notion that the child depends upon particular implements, labelled dangerous, in order to be a danger to himself and other people, is a notion so nonsensical that it is hard to see how any human mind can entertain it for a moment. The truth is that all sorts of faddism, both official and theoretical, have broken down the natural authority of the domestic institution, especially among the poor; and the faddists are now casting about desperately for a substitute for the thing they have themselves destroyed. The normal thing is for the parents to prevent a boy from doing more than a reasonable amount of damage with his bow and arrow; and for the rest, to leave him to a reasonable enjoyment of them. Officialism cannot thus follow the life of the individual boy, as can the individual guardian. You cannot appoint a particular policeman for each boy, to pursue him when he climbs trees or falls into ponds. So the modern spirit has descended to the indescribable mental degradation of trying to abolish the abuse of things by abolishing the things themselves; which is as if it were to abolish ponds or abolish trees. Perhaps it will have a try at that before long. Thus we have all heard of savages who try a tomahawk for murder, or burn a wooden club for the damage it has done to society. To such intellectual levels may the world return.

There are indeed yet lower levels. There is a story from America about a little boy who gave up his toy cannon to assist the disarmament of the world. I do not know if it is true, but on the whole I prefer to think so; for it is perhaps more tolerable to imagine one small monster who could do such a thing than many more mature monsters who could invent or admire it. There were some doubtless who neither invented nor admired. It is one of the peculiarities of the Americans that they combine a power of producing what they satirise as "sob-stuff" with a parallel power of satirising it. And of the two American tall stories, it is sometimes hard to say which is the story and which the satire. But it seems clear that some people did really repeat this story in a reverential spirit. And it marks, as I have said, another stage of cerebral decay. You can (with luck) break a window with a toy arrow; but you can hardly bombard a town with a toy gun. If people object to the mere model of a cannon, they must equally object to the picture of a cannon, and so to every picture in the world that depicts a sword or a spear. There would be a splendid clearance of all the great art-galleries of the world. But it would be nothing to the destruction of all the great libraries of the world, if we logically extended the principle to all the literary masterpieces that admit the glory of arms. When this progress had gone on for a century or two, it might begin to dawn on people that there was something wrong with their moral principle. What is wrong with their moral principle is that it is immoral. Arms, like every other adventure or art of man, have two sides according as they are invoked for the infliction or the defiance of wrong. They have also an element of real poetry and an element of realistic and therefore repulsive prose. The child's symbolic sword and bow are simply the poetry without the prose; the good without the evil. The toy sword is the abstraction and emanation of the heroic, apart from all its horrible accidents. It is the soul of the sword, that will never be stained with blood.

Boyhood and Militarism[*]

What can they mean when they say that we must not put militarism into boys? Can we by any possibility get militarism out of boys? You might burn it out with red-hot irons; you might eventually scourge it out as if it were a mediaeval devil; but except you employ the most poignant form of actual persecution, you certainly will not prevent little boys thinking about soldiers, talking about soldiers, and pretending that they are soldiers.... A child's

[*] Excerpt was originally published in *Illustrated London News*, October 20, 1906.

instinct is almost perfect in the matter of fighting; a child always stands for the good militarism as against the bad. The child's hero is always the man or boy who defends himself suddenly and splendidly against aggression. The child's hero is never the man or boy who attempts by his mere personal force to extend his mere personal influence. In all boys' books, in all boys' conversation, the hero is one person and the bully the other.... To put the matter shortly, a boy feels an abysmal difference between conquest and victory. Conquest has the sound of something cold and heavy; the automatic operations of a powerful army. Victory has the sound of something sudden and valiant; victory is like a cry out of the living mouth. The child is excited with victory; he is bored with conquest.... No; I am not in favour of the child being taught militarism. I am in favour of the child teaching it.

The Child of the Servile State[*]

Now it has hitherto been supposed, in all human laws and customs, that a parent would probably insist on a child being educated, and a parent would probably make an effort to preserve his own child in health. What is quite peculiar to the modern capitalist condition is that for the first time we are assuming, rightly or wrongly, that large numbers of parents will have no such natural affection, and no such normal intelligence. I say rightly or wrongly, for the serious servile deduction remains the same whether we are right or wrong. If we are wrong, they are being driven to be slaves; and if we are right, they deserve to be slaves; but in either case they are or will be slaves. For if you instruct the child's mind in spite of the parent, and take

_____

[*] Excerpt was originally published in *New Witness*, July 9, 1920.

charge of the child's body in spite of the parent, you are taking away not the specialist but the simple functions of a free man. An ordinary man, or even an ordinary animal, cannot do anything more ordinary than rearing his own young. If he cannot do that, he cannot do anything; and if he is not a man he certainly cannot be a citizen. I know he is still given a vote; but that, of course, is because a vote is no longer a value.

The point at present, however, is the sweeping and universal character of the tendency. It is not the exception but the rule. You can make a special law that parents shall not let their children be lashed along dark tunnels tied to a cart, as you can make and do make a special law that they shall not skin their children alive. But like all criminal law, it is based on the assumption that only a select few have a fastidious taste for skinning them alive. Abnormal and atrocious abuse of authority can be punished, and ought to be punished. But this is not a question of the abuse of an authority, but of the abolition of an authority. Coercion so comprehensive as inspection and instruction for a whole populace means that the ordinary man cannot insist on anything for his children's health, and cannot make an effort for anything in his children's education. It no longer means that a few bad men are bad fathers; it means that even good men must be bad fathers. This is the whole point of our protest against various hygenic and philanthropic societies; that they have turned the old exception into a new rule. Many of those movements were started for noble and necessary objects; most of them are still supported by kindly and honourable people. But their little rivulet of reason and goodwill has only gone to swell a torrent with a much deeper channel and much more deadly momentum.

6

Home ... and Work

A Song of Education

I remember my mother, the day that we met,
A thing I shall never entirely forget;
And I toy with the fancy that, young as I am,
I should know her again if we met in a tram.
But mother is happy in turning a crank
That increases the balance at somebody's bank;
And I feel satisfaction that mother is free
From the sinister task of attending to me.

They have brightened our room, that is spacious
    and cool,
With diagrams used in the Idiot School,
And Books for the Blind that will teach us to see;
But mother is happy, for mother is free.
For mother is dancing up forty-eight floors,
For love of the Leeds International Stores,
And the dame of that faith might perhaps have
    grown cold,
With the care of a baby of seven weeks old.

For mother is happy in greasing a wheel
For somebody else, who is cornering Steel;
And though our one meeting was not very long,
She took the occasion to sing me this song:
"O hush thee, my baby, the time will soon come

When thy sleep will be broken with hooting and
    hum;
There are handles want turning and turning all day,
And knobs to be pressed in the usual way;
O, hush thee, my baby, take rest while I croon,
For Progress comes early, and Freedom too soon."

As long as a window can open it will open on the whole
world. As long as a door can shut, it will shut out the
whole world. The home is not only the greatest of human
institutions, but the most infinite. It is only there that we
find the root, and can radiate in all other directions.

— *New Witness*, April 30, 1914

The business done in the home is nothing less than the
shaping of the bodies and souls of humanity. The family is
the factory that manufactures mankind.

— *New Witness*, November 14, 1919

The disintegration of rational society started in the drift
from the hearth and the family; the solution must be a
drift back.

— *G. K.'s Weekly*, March 30, 1933

What is called the economic independence of women is
the same as what is called the economic wage-slavery of
men. The true progressive mind regards it as one of the
wrongs of workmen and one of the rights of women.

— *Illustrated London News*, April 21, 1923

A course and cruel system of sacking and sweating and bi-
sexual toil is totally inconsistent with the free family and is
bound to destroy it.

— "A Last Instance", *What's Wrong with the World*

When people said that the hand that rocks the cradle rules the world, they paid a tribute to hundreds of private hands operating in private homes. But if it meant that one hand, by pressing a button, could rock a hundred cradles, it would certainly mean that mothers as a class were having less influence in the state.

— *G. K.'s Weekly*, August 13, 1927

We are in the strict sense conservatives; because we hold that the old creed and culture of Christendom realise for men, relatively to all that is reasonable and possible, the great art of life which we call Liberty. The truth has made us free; the tradition has given to men the sort of liberty they really like; local customs, individual craftsmanship, variety of self-expression, the presence of personality in production, the dignity of the human will. These are expressed in a thousand things, from hospitality to adventure, from parents instructing their own children to children inventing their own games, from the village commune to the vin du pays, from practical jokes to pilgrimages and from patron saints to public-house signs. The mark of all these things is variety and spontaneity, the direct action of the individual soul on the material environment of mankind. The result is a rich complexity of common things, a wealth of work and worship, a treasure which we refuse to abandon and are resolute to defend.

— *G. K.'s Weekly*, June 12, 1926

The critics, who agree with us about fundamental matters of faith and morals, suggest that our scheme is incompatible with economics and politics.... We ask them to remember that when modern conditions are made an obstacle to the Distributist politics about which we do not agree, they are quite as vividly presented as obstacles to the Christian ethics about which we do agree. If the housing conditions can be described as a hindrance to ownership, they are equally eagerly described as a hindrance to marriage. If the congested life of cities be made an argument for Big Business, it can equally be made an argument for Birth Control. If the critics say that conditions of travel and transport suggest of themselves the idea of the division of labour, they also suggest to many the idea of the divorcing of husbands. If it be in any case a difficult task to provide one man with one house, it is daily becoming a more difficult task to keep him to one wife. If the conditions of commerce have already accustomed him to the loss of responsibility as a proprietor, it is equally true that they have already accustomed him to the loss of responsibility as a parent. If it no longer seems unnatural to receive his wages from remote capitalists, there are many cases in which it does not seem unnatural to send his children to heathen and hostile colleges.

— *G. K.'s Weekly*, October 29, 1927

Property is not the same as income; or, in other words, property is not the same as salary. Income or salary may be more or less contributions to property, according to circumstances or inevitable compromises. But going to a Government Department at regular intervals for your salary or soup-ticket is not the primary idea of property; it is not where property starts or where it ends and is fulfilled. It is the idea of something proper to the person and the family, clinging to him in any case by an adhesion older than history and simpler than the complex arrangements of politics.... The difference is between the idea of birds building nests and the idea of birds being all exactly and equally and humanely kept in cages. A bird who never makes a nest is not a complete bird; a man who does not regard the home as more native even than the native land is not a complete man.

— *G. K.'s Weekly*, June 30, 1928

There can be no pretence of liberty when a man is forced by circumstances to work for one master or starve, when the family is constantly menaced by poverty and oppression by the State, when the possession of private property is the privilege not of the many, but of the few.

— *G. K.'s Weekly*, May 30, 1931

I freely admit that many people, even poor people may want to be enslaved; as starving men often sold themselves into slavery in the last days of paganism. Many are preferring the heathen relapse of divorce to the hard and high ideal of loyalty; just as many are preferring the heathen relapse of servile status to the hard and high ideal of liberty.

— *New Witness*, June 3, 1921

The "homespun" ideal [is] the idea that it is better to do things inside rather than outside the frontier or the fence: that we often lose more than we gain by chaffering with strangers, whether they are pedlars on the road or brokers on the Stock Exchange; that there are not only domestic virtues but domestic values, in the sense of utility and beauty, which are best safeguarded by purely domestic traditions; that not only dirty linen, but much more emphatically, clean linen, is best dealt with at home.

— *G. K.'s Weekly*, August 10, 1933

The clue to innumerable modern complications is precisely that the employer must come first, before even the law-giver, before even the policeman. The commercial firm is to be like the feudal group, the near and natural authority under which men and women are to live; a larger family cutting across and destroying the Christian family. As the feudal ethics said that a man must lose hair and hide for his lord, so the servile ethics say that he must lose wife and child for his boss.

— *New Witness*, June 3, 1921

A very hard-working man cannot get tired of his family.
A very hard-working man can hardly get used to them.

— "Ibsen", *A Handful of Authors*

We have ... the misfortune to live in an age of journalese,
in which anything done inside a house is called "drudgery,"
while anything done inside an office is called "enterprise."

— *G. K.'s Weekly*, September 27, 1930

The healthiest institutions do not eliminate human sin.
But surely there are no such things as healthy institutions,
as distinct from unhealthy ones. There is such a thing as
using sex and property in a sane and fruitful way, instead
of a feverish and fruitless way. A peasant produces and
protects something real; as marriage produces and protects
children.

— *The Observer*, November 30, 1919

The chief charm of having a home that is secure is having
leisure to feel it as strange.

— "The Root of Reality",
Irish Impressions

Happy is he who still loves something that he loved in
the nursery: he has not been broken in two by time; he
is not two men, but one, and has saved not only his soul
but his life.

— *Illustrated London News*,
September 26, 1908

Earth is a task garden; Heaven is a playground.

— "Oxford from Without",
All Things Considered

The Wildness of Domesticity[*]

It is the special psychology of leisure and luxury that falsifies life. Some experience of modern movements of the sort called "advanced" has led me to the conviction that they generally repose upon some experience peculiar to the rich. It is so with that fallacy of free love; the idea of sexuality as a string of episodes. That implies a long holiday in which to get tired of one woman, and a motor car in which to wander looking for others; it also implies money for maintenances. An omnibus conductor has hardly time to love his own wife, let alone other people's. And the success with which nuptial estrangements are depicted in modern problem plays is due to the fact that there is only one thing that a drama cannot depict—that is a hard day's work. I could give many other instances of this plutocratic assumption behind progressive fads. For instance, there is a plutocratic assumption behind the phrase "Why should woman be economically dependent upon man?" The answer is that among poor and practical people she isn't; except in the sense in which he is dependent upon her. A hunter has to tear his clothes; there must be somebody to mend them. A fisher has to catch fish; there must be somebody to cook them. It is surely quite clear that this modern notion that woman is a mere "pretty clinging parasite," "a plaything," etc., arose through the somber contemplation of some rich banking family, in which the banker, at least, went to the city and pretended to do something, while the banker's wife went to the Park and did not pretend to do anything at all. A poor man and his wife are a business partnership. If one partner in a firm of

[*] Excerpt is from "The Wildness of Domesticity", in *What's Wrong with the World*, in *CW* 4:71–74.

publishers interviews the authors while the other inter-
views the clerks, is one of them economically dependent?
Was Hodder a pretty parasite clinging to Stoughton? Was
Marshall a mere plaything for Snelgrove?[1]

But of all the modern notions generated by mere wealth
the worst is this: the notion that domesticity is dull and tame.
Inside the home (they say) is dead decorum and routine;
outside is adventure and variety. This is indeed a rich
man's opinion. The rich man knows that his own house
moves on vast and soundless wheels of wealth, is run by
regiments of servants, by a swift and silent ritual. On the
other hand, every sort of vagabondage of romance is open
to him in the streets outside. He has plenty of money and
can afford to be a tramp. His wildest adventure will end in
a restaurant, while the yokel's tamest adventure may end
in a police-court. If he smashes a window he can pay for it;
if he smashes a man he can pension him. He can (like the
millionaire in the story) buy an hotel to get a glass of gin.
And because he, the luxurious man, dictates the tone of
nearly all "advanced" and "progressive" thought, we have
almost forgotten what a home really means to the overwhelming millions of mankind.

For the truth is, that to the moderately poor the home is
the only place of liberty. Nay, it is the only place of anarchy. It is the only spot on the earth where a man can alter
arrangements suddenly, make an experiment or indulge in
a whim. Everywhere else he goes he must accept the strict
rules of the shop, inn, club, or museum that he happens to
enter. He can eat his meals on the floor in his own house
if he likes. I often do it myself; it gives a curious, childish, poetic, picnic feeling. There would be considerable

---

[1] Hodder and Stoughton are English publishers; Marshall and Snelgrove are
a chain of British stores.

trouble if I tried to do it in an A. B. C. tea-shop. A man can wear a dressing-gown and slippers in his house; while I am sure that this would not be permitted at the Savoy, though I never actually tested the point. If you go to a restaurant you must drink some of the wines on the wine list, all of them if you insist, but certainly some of them. But if you have a house and garden you can try to make hollyhock tea or convolvulus wine if you like. For a plain, hard-working man the home is not the one tame place in the world of adventure. It is the one wild place in the world of rules and set tasks. The home is the one place where he can put the carpet on the ceiling or the slates on the floor if he wants to. When a man spends every night staggering from bar to bar or from music-hall to music-hall, we say that he is living an irregular life. But he is not; he is living a highly regular life, under the dull, and often oppressive, laws of such places. Sometimes he is not allowed even to sit down in the bars; and frequently he is not allowed to sing in the music-halls. Hotels may be defined as places where you are forced to dress; and theaters may be defined as places where you are forbidden to smoke. A man can only picnic at home.

Now I take, as I have said, this small human omnipotence, this possession of a definite cell or chamber of liberty, as the working model for the present inquiry. Whether we can give every Englishman a free home of his own or not, at least we should desire it; and he desires it. For the moment we speak of what he wants, not of what he expects to get. He wants, for instance, a separate house; he does not want a semi-detached house. He may be forced in the commercial race to share one wall with another man. Similarly he might be forced in a three-legged race to share one leg with another man; but it is not so that he pictures himself in his dreams of elegance and liberty. Again, he does not desire a flat. He can eat and sleep and praise God in a flat; he can eat and sleep and praise God in a railway train. But a railway train is not a house, because it is a house on wheels. And a flat is not a house, because it is a house on stilts. An idea of earthy contact and foundation, as well as an idea of separation and independence, is a part of this instructive human picture.

I take, then, this one institution as a test. As every normal man desires a woman, and children born of a woman, every normal man desires a house of his own to put them into. He does not merely want a roof above him and a chair below him; he wants an objective and visible kingdom; a fire at which he can cook what food he likes, a door he can open to what friends he chooses. This is the normal appetite of men; I do not say there are not exceptions. There may be saints above the need and philanthropists below it. Opalstein, now he is a duke, may have got used to more than this; and when he was a convict may have got used to less. But the normality of the thing is enormous. To give nearly everybody ordinary houses would please nearly everybody; that is what I assert without apology. Now in modern England (as you eagerly point out) it is very difficult to give nearly everybody houses. Quite so; I merely set up the *desideratum*; and ask the reader to leave it standing there while he turns with me to a consideration of what really happens in the social wars of our time.

The Drift from Domesticity[*]

In the matter of reforming things, as distinct from deforming them, there is one plain and simple principle; a principle

---

[*] "The Drift from Domesticity", in *The Thing*, in *CW* 3:157–64.

which will probably be called a paradox. There exists in such a case a certain institution or law; let us say, for the sake of simplicity, a fence or gate erected across a road. The more modern type of reformer goes gaily up to it and says, "I don't see the use of this; let us clear it away." To which the more intelligent type of reformer will do well to answer: "If you don't see the use of it, I certainly won't let you clear it away. Go away and think. Then, when you can come back and tell me that you *do* see the use of it, I may allow you to destroy it."

This paradox rests on the most elementary common sense. The gate or fence did not grow there. It was not set up by somnambulists who built it in their sleep. It is highly improbable that it was put there by escaped lunatics who were for some reason loose in the street. Some person had some reason for thinking it would be a good thing for somebody. And until we know what the reason was, we really cannot judge whether the reason was reasonable. It is extremely probable that we have overlooked some whole aspect of the question, if something set up by human beings like ourselves seems to be entirely meaningless and mysterious. There are reformers who get over this difficulty by assuming that all their fathers were fools; but if that be so, we can only say that folly appears to be a hereditary disease. But the truth is that nobody has any business to destroy a social institution until he has really seen it as an historical institution. If he knows how it arose, and what purposes it was supposed to serve, he may really be able to say that they were bad purposes, or that they have since become bad purposes, or that they are purposes which are no longer served. But if he simply stares at the thing as a senseless monstrosity that has somehow sprung up in his path, it is he and not the traditionalist who is suffering from an illusion. We might even say that he is seeing things in a nightmare. This principle applies to a thousand things, to trifles as well as true institutions, to convention as well as to conviction. It was exactly the sort of person, like Joan of Arc, who did know why women wore skirts, who was most justified in not wearing one; it was exactly the sort of person like St. Francis, who did sympathize with the feast and the fireside, who was most entitled to become a beggar on the open road. And when, in the general emancipation of modern society, the Duchess says she does not see why she shouldn't play leapfrog, or the Dean declares that he sees no valid canonical reason why he should not stand on his head, we may say to these persons with patient benevolence: "Defer, therefore, the operation you contemplate until you have realized by ripe reflection what principle or prejudice you are violating. Then play leapfrog and stand on your head and the Lord be with you."

Among the traditions that are being thus attacked, not intelligently but most unintelligently, is the fundamental human creation called the Household or the Home. That is a typical thing which men attack, not because they can see through it, but because they cannot see it at all. They beat at it blindly, in a fashion entirely haphazard and opportunist; and many of them would pull it down without even pausing to ask why it was ever put up. It is true that only a few of them would have avowed this object in so many words. That only proves how very blind and blundering they are. But they have fallen into a habit of mere drift and gradual detachment from family life; something that is often merely accidental and devoid of any definite theory at all. But though it is accidental it is none the less anarchical. And it is all the more anarchical for not being anarchist. It seems to be largely founded on individual irritation; an irritation which varies with the individual. We are merely told that in this or that case a particular temperament was tormented by a particular environment; but nobody even explained how the evil arose, let alone whether the evil is really escaped. We are told that in this or that family Grandmamma talked a great deal of nonsense, which God know is true; or that it is very difficult to have intimate intellectual relations with Uncle Gregory without telling him he is a fool, which is indeed the case. But nobody seriously considers the remedy, or even the malady; or whether the existing individualistic dissolution is a remedy at all. Much of this business began with the influence of Ibsen, a very powerful dramatist and an exceedingly feeble philosopher. I suppose that Nora of The Doll's House was intended to be an inconsequent person; but certainly her most inconsequent action was her last. She complained that she was not yet fit to look after children, and then proceeded to get as far as possible from the children, that she might study them more closely.

There is one simple test and type of this neglect of scientific thinking and the sense of a social rule; the neglect which has now left us with nothing but a welter of exceptions. I have read hundreds and thousands of times, in all the novels and newspapers of our epoch, certain phrases about the just right of the young to liberty, about the unjust claim of the elders to control, about the conception that all souls must be free or all citizens equal, about the absurdity of authority or the degradation of obedience. I am not arguing those matters directly at the moment. But what strikes me as astounding, in a logical sense, is that not one of these myriad novelists and newspaper-men ever seems to think of asking the next and most obvious question. It never seems to occur to them to inquire what becomes of the opposite obligation. If the child is free from the first to disregard the parent, why is not the parent free from the first to disregard the child? If Mr. Jones, Senior, and Mr. Jones, junior, are only two free and equal citizens, why should one citizen sponge on another citizen for the first fifteen years of his life? Why should the elder Mr. Jones be expected to feed, clothe and shelter out of his own pocket another person who is entirely free of any obligations to him? If the bright young thing cannot be asked to tolerate her grandmother, who has become something of a bore, why should the grandmother or the mother have tolerated the bright young thing at a period of her life when she was by no means bright? Why did they laboriously look after her at a time when her contributions to the conversation were seldom epigrammatic and not often intelligible? Why should Jones Senior stand drinks and free meals to anybody so unpleasant as Jones Junior, especially in the immature phases of his existence? Why should he not throw the baby out of the window; or at any rate, kick the boy out of doors? It is obvious that we are dealing with a real relation, which may be equality, but is certainly not similarity.

Some social reformers try to evade this difficulty, I know, by some vague notions about the State or an abstraction called Education eliminating the parental function. But this, like many notions of solid scientific persons, is a wild illusion of the nature of mere moonshine. It is based on that strange new superstition, the idea of infinite resources of organization. It is as if officials grew like grass or bred like rabbits. There is supposed to be an endless supply of salaried persons, and of salaries for them; and they are to undertake all that human beings naturally do for themselves; including the care of children. But men cannot live by taking in each other's baby-linen. They cannot provide a tutor for each citizen; who is to tutor the tutors? Men cannot be educated by machinery; and though there might be a Robot bricklayer or scavenger, there will never be a

Robot schoolmaster or governess. The actual effect of this theory is that one harassed person has to look after a hundred children, instead of one normal person looking after a normal number of them. Normally that normal person is urged by a natural force, which costs nothing and does not require a salary; the force of natural affection for his young, which exists even among the animals. If you cut off that natural force, and substitute a paid bureaucracy, you are like a fool who should pay men to turn the wheel of his mill, because he refused to use wind or water which he could get for nothing. You are like a lunatic who should carefully water his garden with a watering-can, while holding up an umbrella to keep off the rain.

It is now necessary to recite these truisms; for only by doing so can we begin to get a glimpse of that *reason* for the existence of the family, which I began this essay by demanding. They were all familiar to our fathers, who believed in the links of kinship and also in the links of logic. Today our logic consists mostly of missing links; and our family largely of absent members. But, anyhow, this is the right end at which to begin any such inquiry; and *not* at the tail-end or the fag-end of some private muddle, by which Dick has become discontented or Susan has gone off on her own. If Dick or Susan wish to destroy the family because they do not see the use of it, I say as I said in the beginning; if they do not see the use of it, they had much better preserve it. They have no business even to think of destroying it until they have seen the use of it.

But it has other uses, besides the obvious fact that it means a necessary social work being done for love when it cannot be done for money; and (one might almost dare to hint) presumably to be repaid with love since it is never repaid in money. On that simple side of the matter the general situation is easy to record. The existing and general system of society, subject in our own age and industrial culture to very gross abuses and painful problems, is nevertheless a normal one. It is the idea that the commonwealth is made up of a number of small kingdoms, of which a man and a woman become the king and queen and in which they exercise a reasonable authority, subject to the common sense of the commonwealth, until those under their care grow up to found similar kingdoms and exercise similar authority. This is the social structure of mankind, far older than all its records and more universal than any of its religions; and all attempts to alter it are mere talk and tomfoolery.

But the other advantage of the small group is now not so much neglected as simply not realized. Here again we have some extraordinary delusions spread all over the literature and journalism of our time. Those delusions now exist in such a degree that we may say, for all practical purposes, that when a thing has been stated about a thousand times as obviously true, it is almost certain to be obviously false. One such statement may be specially noted here. There is undoubtedly something to be said against domesticity and in favour of the general drift towards life in hotels, clubs, colleges, communal settlements and the rest; or for a social life organized on the plan of the great commercial system of our time. But the truly extraordinary suggestion is often made that this escape from the home is an escape into greater freedom. The change is actually offered as favourable to liberty.

To anybody who can think, of course, it is exactly the opposite. The domestic division of human society is not perfect, being human. It does not achieve complete liberty; a thing somewhat difficult to do or even to define. But it is a mere matter of arithmetic that it puts a larger number of people in supreme control of something, and able to shape it to their personal liking, than do the vast organizations that rule society outside; whether those systems are legal or commercial or even merely social. Even if we were only considering the parents, it is plain that there are more parents than there are policemen or politicians or heads of big businesses or proprietors of hotels. As I shall suggest in a moment, the argument actually applies indirectly to the children as well as directly to the parents. But the main point is that the world *outside* the home is now under a rigid discipline and routine and it is only inside the home that there is really a place for individuality and liberty. Anyone stepping out of the front-door is obliged to step into a procession, all going the same way and to a great extent even obliged to wear the same uniform. Business, especially big business, is now organized like an army. It is, as some would say, a sort of mild militarism without bloodshed; as I should say, a militarism without the military virtues. But anyhow, it is obvious that a hundred clerks in a bank or a hundred waitresses in a teashop are more regimented and under rule than the same individuals when each has gone back to his or her own dwelling or lodging, hung with his or her favourite pictures or fragrant with his or her favourite cheap cigarettes. But this, which is so obvious in the commercial case, is no less true even in the social case. In practice, the pursuit of pleasure is merely the pursuit of fashion. The pursuit of fashion is merely the pursuit of convention; only that it happens to be a new convention. The jazz dances, the joy rides, the big pleasure parties and hotel entertainments, do not make any more provision for a *really* independent taste than did any of the fashions of the past. If a wealthy young lady wants to do what all the other wealthy young ladies are doing, she will find it great fun, simply because youth is fun and society is fun. She will enjoy being modern exactly as her Victorian grandmother enjoyed being Victorian. And quite right too; but it is the enjoyment of convention, not the enjoyment of liberty. It is perfectly healthy for all young people of all historic periods to herd together, to a reasonable extent, and enthusiastically copy each other. But in that there is nothing particularly fresh and certainly nothing particularly free. The girl who likes shaving her head and powdering her nose and wearing short skirts will find the world organized for her and will march happily with the procession. But a girl who happened to like having her hair down to her heels or loading herself with barbaric gauds and trailing garments or (most awful of all) leaving her nose in its natural state—she will still be well advised to do these things on her own premises. If the Duchess does want to play leapfrog, she must not start suddenly leaping in the manner of a frog across the ballroom of the Babylon Hotel, when it is crowded with the fifty best couples professionally practising the very latest dance, for the instruction of society. The Duchess will find it easier to practice leapfrog to the admiration of her intimate friends in the old oak-panelled hall of Fitzdragon Castle. If the Dean must stand on his head, he will do it with more ease and grace in the calm atmosphere of the Deanery than by attempting to interrupt the program of some social entertainment already organized for philanthropic purposes.

If there is this impersonal routine in commercial and even in social things, it goes without saying that it exists and always must exist in political and legal things. For instance, the punishments of the State must be sweeping generalizations. It is only the punishments of the home that can possibly be adapted to the individual case; because it is only there that the judge can know anything of the individual. If Tommy takes a silver thimble out of a work-basket, his mother may act very differently according as she knows that he did it for fun or for spite or to sell to somebody, or to get somebody into trouble. But if Tomkins takes a silver thimble out of a shop, the law not only can but must punish him according to the rule made for all shoplifters or stealers of silver. It is only the domestic discipline that can show any sympathy or especially any humour. I do not say that the family always does do this: but I say that the state never ought to attempt it. So that even if we consider the parents alone as independent princes, and the children merely as subjects, the relative freedom of the family can and often does work to the advantage of those subjects. But so long as the children are children, they will always be the subjects of somebody. The question is whether they are to be distributed naturally under their natural princes, as the old phrase went, who normally feel for them what nobody else will feel, a natural affection. It seems to me clear that this normal distribution gives the largest amount of liberty to the largest number of people.

My complaint of the anti-domestic drift is that it is unintelligent. People do not know what they are doing; because they do not know what they are undoing. There are a multitude of modern manifestations, from the largest to the smallest, ranging from a divorce to a picnic party. But each is a separate escape or evasion; and especially an evasion of the point at issue. People ought to decide in a philosophical fashion whether they desire the traditional social order or not; or if there is any particular alternative to be desired. As it is they treat the public question merely as a mess or medley of private questions. Even in being anti-domestic they are much too domestic in their test of domesticity. Each family considers only its own case and the result is merely narrow and negative. Each case is an exception to a rule that does not exist. The family, especially in the modern state, stands in need of considerable correction and reconstruction; most things do in the modern state. But the family mansion should be preserved or destroyed or rebuilt; it should not be allowed to fall to pieces brick by brick because nobody has any historic sense of the object of bricklaying. For instance, the architects of the restoration should rebuild the house with wide and easily opened doors, for the practice of the ancient virtue of hospitality. In other words, private property should be distributed with sufficiently decent equality to allow of a margin for festive intercourse. But the hospitality of a house will always be different from the hospitality of a hotel. And it will be different in being more individual, more independent, more interesting than the hospitality of a hotel. It is perfectly right that the young Browns and the young Robinsons should meet and mix and dance and make asses of themselves, according to the design of their Creator. But there will always be some difference between the Browns entertaining the Robinsons and the Robinsons entertaining the Browns. And it will be a difference to the advantage of variety, of personality, of the potentialities of the mind of man; or, in other words, of life, liberty and the pursuit of happiness.

The Emancipation of Domesticity[*]

The wife is like the fire, or to put things in their proper proportion, the fire is like the wife. Like the fire, the woman is expected to cook: not to excel in cooking, but to cook; to cook better than her husband who is earning the coke by lecturing on botany or breaking stones. Like

[*] Excerpt is from "The Emancipation of Domesticity", in *What's Wrong with the World*, in *CW* 4:115–19.

the fire, the woman is expected to tell tales to the children, not original and artistic tales, but tales—better tales than would probably be told by a first-class cook. Like the fire, the woman is expected to illuminate and ventilate, not by the most startling revelations or the wildest winds of thought, but better than a man can do it after breaking stones or lecturing. But she cannot be expected to endure anything like this universal duty if she is also to endure the direct cruelty of competitive or bureaucratic toil. Woman must be a cook, but not a competitive cook; a school mistress, but not a competitive schoolmistress; a house-decorator but not a competitive house-decorator; a dress-maker, but not a competitive dressmaker. She should have not one trade but twenty hobbies; she, unlike the man, may develop all her second bests. This is what has been really aimed at from the first in what is called the seclusion, or even the oppression, of women. Women were not kept at home in order to keep them narrow; on the contrary, they were kept at home in order to keep them broad. The world outside the home was one mass of narrowness, a maze of cramped paths, a madhouse of monomaniacs. It was only by partly limiting and protecting the woman that she was enabled to play at five or six professions and so come almost as near to God as the child when he plays at a hundred trades. But the woman's professions, unlike the child's, were all truly and almost terribly fruitful; so tragically real that nothing but her universality and balance prevented them being merely morbid. I do not deny that women have been wronged and even tortured; but I doubt if they were ever tortured so much as they are tortured now by the absurd modern attempt to make them domestic empresses and competitive clerks at the same time. I do not deny that even under the old tradition women had a harder time than men; that is why we take off our hats. I do not deny that all these various female functions were exasperating; but I say that there was some aim and meaning in keeping them various. . . .

The shortest way of summarizing the position is to say that woman stands for the idea of Sanity; that intellectual home to which the mind must return after every excursion or extravagance. The mind that finds its way to wild places is the poet's; but the mind that never finds its way back is the lunatic's. . . .

. . . Supposing it to be conceded that humanity has acted at least not unnaturally in dividing itself into two halves, it is not difficult to see why the line of cleavage has followed the line of sex, or why the female became the emblem of the universal and the male of the special. A gigantic fact of nature fixed it thus: it surrounded the woman with very young children, who require to be taught not so much anything as everything. Babies need not to be taught a trade, but to be introduced to a world. To put the matter shortly, woman is generally shut up in a house with a human being at the time when he asks all the questions that there are, and some that there aren't. It would be odd if she retained any of the narrowness of a specialist. Now if anyone says that this duty of general enlightenment is oppressive, I can understand the view. I can only answer that our race has thought it worth while to cast this burden on women in order to keep common-sense in the world. But when people begin to talk about this domestic duty as not merely difficult but trivial and dreary, I simply give up the question. For I cannot with the utmost energy of imagination conceive what they mean. When domesticity, for instance, is called drudgery, all the difficulty arises from a double meaning in the word. If drudgery only means dreadfully hard work, I admit the woman drudges in the home, as a man might drudge at the Cathedral of Amiens

or drudge behind a gun at Trafalgar. But if it means that
the hard work is more heavy because it is trifling, colorless
and of small import to the soul, then as I say, I give it up;
I do not know what the words mean. To be Queen Elizabeth within a definite area, deciding sales, banquets, labors
and holidays; to be Aristotle within a certain area, teaching
morals, manners, theology, and hygiene; I can understand
how this might exhaust the mind, but I cannot imagine
how it could narrow it. How can it be a large career to
tell other people's children about the Rule of Three, and a
small career to tell one's own children about the universe?
How can it be broad to be the same thing to everyone,
and narrow to be everything to someone? No; a woman's
function is laborious, but because it is gigantic, not because
it is minute. I will pity Mrs. Jones for the hugeness of her
task; I will never pity her for its smallness. . . .

The Dignity of Domesticity[*]

Modern moral controversy reels to and fro, to such an
extent that men seem sometimes to change weapons, as
in the duel in *Hamlet*, or even change places, as in the
game of Puss-in-the-Corner. It would seem that in a
recent discussion on that totally new topic, the True Position of Woman, some rather remarkable manifestations
were made. It seems that Mr. Henry Ford, the very incar-
nation of swift progress and practical industrialism, has
been saying that Woman's only place is the Home. And
it seems that Mr. Bertrand Russell, the very champion
of Feminism, has been saying that American civilization

* Excerpt was originally published in *Illustrated London News*, November 16,
1929.

is over-feminised. The report in question sums up his view by saying that "American women are over-romantic, and that the American family is disintegrating in consequence, since it is regarded primarily as the vehicle of sentimental compatibility and not as a child-rearing unit." The language is a little pedantic; but on the whole it serves to show that everybody has a sane spot somewhere, even Cambridge philosophers and scientific millionaires. But the philosopher is more philosophical than the millionaire, for it is the wrong way of putting it to say that Woman should be confined to the Home, as if it were a Home for Incurables. The Home is not a prison, or even an asylum; nor is the case for the Home the idea that certain people should be locked up in it because they are weak-minded or incapable. It is as if men had said that the Priestess of Delphi should be kept in her place, which was to sit on a tripod and deliver nice little oracles. Or it is as if Miss Maude Royden[2] were accused of saying that a woman should be locked up in the pulpit and not allowed to pollute the rest of the church. Those who believe in the dignity of the domestic tradition, who happen to be the overwhelming majority of mankind, regard the home as a sphere of vast social importance and supreme spiritual significance; and to talk of being confined to it is like talking of being chained to a throne, or set in the seat of judgment as if it were the stocks. There may be women who are uncomfortable in family life, as there have certainly been men who were uncomfortable on thrones. There are wives who do not want to be mothers; and there are lawyers who do not want to be judges. But, taking normal human nature and historic tradition as a whole, we cannot be expected to start the discussion by assuming that these

[2] Royden (1876–1956) was a social worker who was very active in the suffrage movement. As an assistant preacher at a London church, she was the first woman in England to speak from a pulpit on a regular basis.

human dignities are not the object of human desires. We cannot simply take it for granted that kings are humiliated by being crowned. We cannot accept it as a first principle that a man is made a judge because he is a fool. And we cannot assume, as both sides in this curious controversy so often do assume, that bringing forth and rearing and ruling the living beings of the future is a servile task suited to a silly person.

It is, however, a curious example of the way in which a modern tendency will often cut its own throat. People begin by saying that it is an antiquated tyranny to ask women to form part of "a child-rearing unit." They encourage them to talk sham psychology about compatibility and affinity, and all the rest of it, with the result, as Mr. Bertrand Russell sees, that the view of the whole thing becomes pestiferously sentimental. Then they find that, in introducing the New Woman who shall appeal to posterity, they have in fact introduced a very old-fashioned sort of woman, as fastidious, hysterical, and irresponsible as any silly spinster in a Victorian novel; and, above all, that, so far as she is concerned, there is no posterity to appeal to. Meanwhile, by this ingenious *detour*, they have managed to lose the other opportunity altogether. They cannot get the female energy harnessed again to the human and creative purposes of the family, because they have started by denouncing and deriding those purposes as slavish and superstitious. They began by saying that only silly women were domestic; then they went off with the sensible women and watched them turning silly; and now they cannot get anybody to go in for what they originally deprecated as silliness. It is as if they had spat upon all work as being servile work, created a whole generation that could do no work, and then clamoured in vain for somebody to do the work although it was servile. There is no hope for them, except to begin again at the beginning;

and consider the paradox that free men can labour or that free women can be at home, even at home.

I have never understood myself how this superstition arose: the notion that a woman plays a lowly part in the home and a loftier part outside the home. There may be all sorts of excellent reasons for individuals doing or not doing either; but I cannot understand how the domestic thing can be considered inferior in the nature of the thing done. Most work done in the outer world is pretty mechanical work; some of it is decidedly dirty work. There seems no possible sense in which it is intrinsically superior to domestic work. Nine times out of ten, the only difference is that the one person is drudging for people she does care for and the other drudging for people she does not care for. But, allowing for the element of drudgery in both cases, there is rather more element of distinction in the domestic case. The most fully trusted official must very largely go by rules and regulations established by superiors. The mother of a family makes her own rules and regulations; and they are not merely mechanical rules, but often very fundamental moral rules. Nor are they merely monotonous in their application. Mr. Ford is reported, rightly or wrongly, as saying that the woman should not be in the business of the outer world, because business people have to make decisions. I should say that mothers have to make many more decisions. A great part of a big business goes by routine; and all the technical part of Mr. Ford's business goes, quite literally, on oiled wheels. It is the very boast of such a system that its products are made rapidly because rigidly, upon a regular pattern, and can be trusted ninety-nine times out of a hundred to turn out according to plan. But a little boy does not, by any means, always turn out according to plan. The little boy will present a series of problems in the course of twenty-four hours which would correspond to a Ford car bursting like a bomb or flying out of the window like an aeroplane. The little boy is individual; he cannot be mended with spare parts from another little boy. The mother cannot order another little boy at the same works, and make the experiment work. The domestic woman really is called upon to make decisions, real or moral decisions, and she jolly well does. Some have even complained that her decisions were too decisive.

I suppose the prejudice must have sprung merely from the fact that domestic operations occur in a small space, and on private premises. Even that is illogical enough, in an age that is so proud of the experimental history of science. The most epoch-making scientific feats have been performed in a space no larger than a parlour or a nursery. A baby is bigger than a bacillus: and even the little boy is larger and more lively than a germ under the microscope. And the science that is studied in the home is the greatest and most glorious of all sciences, very inadequately indicated by the word education, and nothing less, at least, than the mystery of the making of men. It does not seem to me in the least odd that so mysterious and momentous a business should have been surrounded by virtues of vigilance and loyalty, as by an armed guard; or that the partners in it should have a sealed and sacred relationship. We may or may not be content with the frigid phrase that the family is a child-rearing unit. But it is not unreasonable to expect a unit to have unity.

Women in the Workplace—and in the Home[*]

The recent controversy about the professional position of married women was part of a much larger controversy, which is not limited to professional women or even to

[*]Excerpt was originally published in *Illustrated London News*, December 18, 1926.

women. It involves a distinction that controversialists on both sides commonly forget. As it is conducted, it turns largely on the query about whether family life is what is called a "whole-time job" or a "half-time job." But there is also another distinction between a whole job and a half job, or a hundredth part of a job. It has nothing to do with the time that is occupied, but only with the ground that is covered. An industrial expert once actually boasted that it took twenty men to make a pin; and I hope he sat down on the pin. But the man making the twentieth part of the pin did not only work for the twentieth part of an hour. He might perfectly well be working for twelve hours—indeed, he might have been working for twenty-four hours for all the happy industrial expert generally cared. He might work for the whole of a lifetime, but he never made the whole of a pin.

Now, there are lingering still in the world a number of lunatics, among whom I have the honour to count myself, who think it a good thing to preserve as many whole jobs as possible. We congratulate ourselves, in our crazy fashion, whenever we find anybody personally and completely doing anything. We rejoice when we find remaining in the world any cases in which the individual can see the beginning and the end of his own work. We are well aware that this is often incompatible with modern scientific civilization, and the fact has sometimes moved us to say what we think about modern scientific civilization. But anyhow, whether we are right or wrong, that is an important distinction not always remembered; and that is the important distinction that ought to be most remembered, and is least remembered, in this modern debate about the occupation of women.

Probably there must be a certain number of people doing work which they do not complete. Perhaps there must be some people doing work which they do not comprehend. But we do not want to multiply those people indefinitely, and then cover it all by shouting about emancipation and equality. It may be emancipation to allow a woman to make part of a pin, if she really wants to make part of a pin. It may be equality if she is really filled with a furious jealousy of her husband, who has the privilege of making part of a pin. But we question whether it is really a more human achievement to make part of a pin than to make the whole of a pinafore [an apron-like dress]. And we even go further, and question whether it is more human to make the whole of a pinafore than to look after the whole of a child. The point about the "half-time job" of motherhood is that it is at least one of the jobs that can be regarded as a whole, and almost as an end in itself. A human being is in some sense an end in himself. Anything that makes him happy or high-minded is, under God, a thing directed to an ultimate end. It is not, like nearly all the trades and professions, merely a machinery and a means to an end. And it is a thing which can, by the constitution of human nature, be pursued with positive and unpurchased enthusiasm. Whether or no it is a half-time job, it need not be a half-hearted job.

Now, as a matter of fact, there are not so many jobs which normal and ordinary people can pursue with enthusiasm for their own sakes. The position is generally falsified by quoting the exceptional cases of specialists who achieve success. There may be a woman who is so very fond of swimming the Channel that she can go on doing it until she breaks a record. There may be, for that matter, a woman who is so fond of discovering the North Pole that she goes on doing it long after it has been discovered. Such sensational successes naturally bulk big in the newspapers, because they are sensational cases. But they are not the question of whether women are more free in professional or domestic life. To answer that question, we must assume all the sailors on the Channel boats to be women, all the fishermen in the herring fleet to be women, all the whalers in the North Sea to be women, and then consider whether the worst paid and hardest worked of all those workers were really having a happier or a harder life. It will be at once apparent that the vast majority of them must be under orders; and that perhaps a considerable minority of them would be under orders which they did not entirely understand. There could not be a community in which the average woman was in command of a ship. But there can be a community in which the average woman is in command of a house.

To take a hundred women out of a hundred houses and give them a hundred ships would be obviously impossible, unless all the ships were canoes. And that would be carrying to rather fanatical lengths the individualist ideal of people paddling their own canoe. To take the hundred women out of the hundred houses and put them on ten ships, or more probably on two ships, is obviously to increase vastly the number of servants and diminish the number of mistresses.

I fear that the experience of most subordinate women in shops and factories is a little more strenuous. I have taken an extremely elementary and crude example, but I am not the first rhetorician who has found it convenient to discuss the State under the bright and original similitude of a ship. But the principle does apply quite as much to a shop as to a ship. It applies with especial exactitude to the modern shop, which is almost larger than the modern ship. A shop or a factory must consist of a very large majority of servants; and one of the few human institutions in which there need be no such enormous majority of servants is the human household. I still think, therefore, that for the lady interested in ships the most supreme and symbolical moment is the moment when her ships come home. And I think there are some sort of symbolical ships that had much better come home and stay there.

I know all about the necessary modifications and compromises produced by the accidental conditions of to-day. I am not unreasonable about them. But what we are discussing is not the suggestion that the ideal should be modified. It is the suggestion that the ideal should be abolished. It is the suggestion that a new test or method of judgment should be applied to the affair, which is not the test of whether the thing is a whole job, in the sense of a self-sufficing and satisfactory job, but of whether it is what is called a half-time job—that is, a thing to be measured by the mechanical calculation of modern employment.

There have been household gods and household saints and household fairies. I am not sure that there have yet been any factory gods or factory saints or factory fairies. I may be wrong, as I am no commercial expert, but I have not heard of them as yet. And we think that the reason lies in the distinction which I made at the beginning of these remarks. The imagination and the religious instinct and the human sense of humour have free play when people are dealing with something which, however small, is rounded and complete like a cosmos.

The place where babies are born, where men die, where the drama of mortal life is acted, is not an office or a shop or a bureau. It is something much smaller in size and much larger in scope. And while nobody would be such a fool as to pretend that it is the only place where people should work, or even the only place where women should work, it has a character of unity and universality that is not found in any of the fragmentary experiences of the division of labour.

224

The Feminist and the Factory[*]

Loyalty in the family is the chief security for liberty in the state. It is the one voluntary organisation in the world that is coming more and more to consist of compulsory organisations.... This free institution ... is founded on attraction....

The family is based on the astounding fact that an ordinary person does actually prefer to trust a particular individual of the opposite sex, rather than almost impersonal groups even of his (or her) own sex. If the limitation of life require, in certain times or topics, something like economic dependance, something like military command, some favours *pro tem* or some authority *ad hoc*, the human being (incredible as it seems) does prefer to have these things from another human being chosen out of all humanity, rather than from a gang of brutal capitalists or corrupt politicians. What is called the economic independence of women simply means their economic dependence on the capitalists, or the politicians who are the puppets of the capitalists. Now, of course it is perfectly true, in one sense, that if any woman likes this she is at liberty to take it; and that her opportunity may be described as liberty. And it is equally true that any woman who wishes to run away, and form part of the harem of the Grand Turk, may in one sense describe her choice as liberty. Some are actually attracted, it is said, to Mormonism.... Their choice would still in this sense be liberty. But when we are by hypothesis supporting or denouncing social tendencies of our time, we are obviously entitled to say that this form of liberty is a form of suicide. We are surely justified in pointing out that the Mormon or the Moslem does not give so much

[*] Excerpt was originally published in *New Witness*, November 5, 1920.

freedom to woman as the Christian. We have a right to say that whether or no there is enough freedom in the household, there is less in the harem.... And what I should say of the unchivalrous ethics of polygamy, I should also say of the unchivalrous and inhuman ethics of modern commerce. Women are herded and ordered about in a factory exactly as they herded and ordered about in a harem; and what is common to both is the absence of a certain type of individual dignity that is possible in a household. I do not say the home is a place where the woman as such is always respected; for human folly and wickedness will creep in to any social arrangement old or new. But I do say it is a place where the woman as such can be respected; and that the marts of modern capitalism are places where she not only is not, but cannot possibly be. We are therefore in favour of everything that makes the family independent and united, and especially of that idea of the private property of the family, which prevents the capitalist from breaking it up, and selling its separate members into slavery.

A Feminist Fallacy[*]

Through vast quantities of feminist literature there runs one simple but far-reaching fallacy. The case for what is called the "Emancipation of Women" rests on a false analogy between the division of the sexes and other divisions, such as that between rich and poor, slave and free, nation and nation, or class and class. But there is no analogy between sex and anything else in this world: it is entirely unique, because it is a separation which results in an attraction. You cannot say, "Women are under men as negroes

[*] Excerpt was originally published in *Illustrated London News*, April 29, 1911.

are under white men, or Irishmen under Englishmen."
It is not true; and however much women are practically
oppressed, it is still not true. The sexes tend, without any
coercion, to come together. Consequently, in all moralis-
ing or legislating about sex, we must constantly allow for
an element that does not exist in any other caste, section,
or division.

No tyrants wish to please their slaves, and few sensible
slaves do much to please their tyrants; and for this reason
men and women never have been, and never can be, *merely*
in the relation of tyrants and slaves. There may have been
a good deal of tyranny mixed up with it; there has been,
and not male tyranny only. But this evil element can never
be detected or destroyed but by a sane analysis, which will
also recognise the element of inevitable attraction. Marriage is not a hammer, but a magnet. The family does not
rest on force, but on sex. And the upshot of it is that most
of the ancient customs of the sexes are conveniences: not
things imposed by one party, but things equally desired by
both. I am not here speaking of laws and statutes (many of
which, I think, are really unjust), but of certain deep and
tenacious human habits, as the disproportionate emphasis
on bodily dignity in the female or bodily hardihood in the
male. These were never imposed; they are the oldest and
freest things in the world.

Head of the House[*]

The man is the head of the house, while the woman is the
heart of the house. The definition of the head is that it
is the thing that talks. The head of an arrow is not more

---

[*] Excerpt was originally published in *Illustrated London News*, April 22, 1911.

necessary than the shaft of it; perhaps not so much. The head of an axe is not more necessary than the handle; for mere fighting I would sooner have the handle alone than the blade alone. But the head of axe and arrow is the thing that enters first; the thing that speaks. If I kill a man with an arrow I send the arrow-head as an ambassador, to open the question. If I split a man's skull with an axe, it is the blade of the axe that opens the question—and the head.

Now the old human family, on which all civilisation is built, meant this when it talked about its "head." It has nothing to do with detailed despotism or the control of other people's daily lives. That is quite another and later idea, arising out of the crazy complexity of all high civil-isations. If authority means power (which it does not), I think the wife has more of it than the husband. If I look round any ordinary room at all the objects—at their colour, choice, and place—I feel as if I were a lonely and stranded male in a world wholly made by women.

All the same, if a canvasser comes to urge the cause of the Conservative-Radicals or of the Radical-Conservatives, it is I who ought to see him. If a drunkard has wandered into my front garden and lain down on the principal flower-bed, it is I who ought to inspect him. If a burglar wanders about the house at night, it is I who ought to parley with him. Because I am the head; I am the tiresome excrescence that can talk to the world.

The Equality of Sexlessness[*]

In almost all of the modern opinions on women it is curi-ous to observe how many lies have to be assumed before a

---

[*] Excerpt was originally published in *G. K.'s Weekly*, July 26, 1930.

case can be made. A young lady flies from England to Australia; another wins an air race; a Duchess creates a speed record in reaching India; others win motoring trophies; and now the King's prize for marksmanship has gone to a woman. All of which is very interesting and possibly praiseworthy as means of spending one's leisure; and if it were left at that, even if no more were added than the perfectly plain statement that such feats could not have been achieved by their mothers or their grandmothers, we would be content to doff our hats to the ladies with all the courtesy and respect which courage, endurance and ability have always rightly demanded. But it is not left at that; and considerably more is added. It is suggested, for example, that the tasks were beyond the mothers and the grandmothers, not for the very obvious reason that they had no motorcars and airplanes in which to amuse their leisure hours, but because women were then enslaved by the convention of natural inferiority to man. Those days, we are told, "in which women were held to be incapable of positive social achievements are gone for ever." It does not seem to have occurred to this critic that the very fact of being a mother and a grandmother indicates a certain positive social achievement; the achievement of which, indeed, probably left little leisure for travelling airily about the hemispheres. The same critic goes on to state, with all the solemn emphasis of profound thought, that "the important thing is not that women are the same as men— that is a fallacy—but that they are just as valuable to society as men.... Equality of citizenship means that there are twice as many heads to solve present-day problems as there were to solve the problems of the past. And two heads are better than one." And the dreadful proof of the modern collapse of all that was meant by man and wife and the family council, is that this sort of imbecility can be taken seriously. *The Times*, in a studied leading article, points out that the first emancipators of women (whoever they were) had no idea of what lay in store for future generations. "Could they have foreseen it they might have disarmed much opposition by pointing to the possibilities, not only of freedom, but of equality and fraternity also." And we ask—what does it all mean? What in the name of all that is graceful and dignified does fraternity with women mean? What nonsense, or worse, is indicated by the freedom and the equality of the sexes? We mean something quite definite when we speak of a man being a little free with the ladies. What definite freedom is meant when the freedom of women is proposed? If it merely means the right to free opinions; the right to vote independently of husbands or fathers; what possible connection has it with the freedom to fly to Australia or score bulls-eyes at Bisley? If it really means, as we fear it does, freedom from the responsibility of managing a home and a family, an equal right with men in business and social careers, at the expense of home and family, then such progress we can only call a progressive deterioration. And for men too, there is, according to a famous authoress, a hope of freedom. Men are beginning to revolt, we are told, against the old tribal custom of desiring fatherhood. The male is casting off the shackles of being a creator and a man. When all are sexless there will be equality. There will be no women and no men. There will be but a fraternity, free and equal. The only consoling thought is that it will endure but for one generation.

On Household Gods and Goblins[*]

Sometime ago I went with some children to see Maeterlinck's fine and delicate fairy play about the Blue Bird that

* "On Household Gods and Goblins", *The Coloured Lands* (New York: Sheed and Ward, 1937), pp. 195–200.

brought everybody happiness. For some reason or other it did not bring me happiness, and even the children were not quite happy. I will not go so far as to say that the Blue Bird was a Blue Devil, but it left us in something seriously like the blues. The children were partly dissatisfied with it because it did not end with a Day of Judgment; because it was never revealed to the hero and heroine that the dog had been faithful and the cat faithless. For children are innocent and love justice; while most of us are wicked and naturally prefer mercy.

But there was something wrong about the Blue Bird, even from my more mature and corrupt point of view. There were several incidental things I did not like. I did not like the sentimental passage about the love-affair of two babes unborn; it seemed to me a piece of what may be called bad Barrie; and logically it spoilt the only meaning of the scene, which was that the babes were looking to all earthly experiences as things inconceivable. I was not convinced when the boy exclaimed, "There are no dead," for I am by no means sure that he (or the dramatist) knew what he meant by it. "I heard a voice from Heaven cry: Blessed are the dead ..." [Rev 14:13]. I do not know all that is meant in that; but I think the person who said it knew. But there was something more continuous and clinging in the whole business which left me vaguely restless. And I think the nearest to a definition was that I felt as if the poet was condescending to everything; condescending to pots and pans and birds and beasts and babies.

The one part of the business which I really felt to be original and suggestive was the animation of all the materials of the household, as if with familiar spirits; the spirit of fire, the spirit of water and the rest. And even here I felt a faint difference which moved me to an imaginary comparison. I wonder that none of our medievalists has made a Morality or allegorical play founded on the Canticle of Saint Francis, which speaks somewhat similarly of Brother Fire and Sister Water. It would be a real exercise in Gothic craftsmanship and decoration to make these symbolic figures at once stiff and fantastic. If nobody else does this I shall be driven to spoil the idea myself, as I have spoiled so many other rather good ideas in my time. But the point of the parallel at the moment is merely this: that the medieval poet does strike me as having felt about fire like a child while the modern poet felt about it like a man talking to children.

Few and simple as are the words of the older poem, it does somehow convey to me that when the poet spoke of fire as untameable and strong, he felt it as something that might conceivably be feared as well as loved. I do not think the modern poet feared the nursery fire as a child who loved it might fear it. And this elemental quality in the real primitives brought back to my mind something I have always felt about this conception, which is the really fine conception in the Blue Bird: I mean something like that which the heathens embodied in the images of the household gods. The household gods, I believe, were carved out of wood; which makes them even more like the chairs and tables.

The nomad and the anarchist accuse the domestic ideal of being merely timid and prim. But this is not because they themselves are bolder or more vigorous, but simply because they do not know it well enough to know how bold and vigorous it is. The most nomadic life to-day is not the life of the desert but of the industrial cities. They live in clubs and hotels and are often simply ignorant, I might almost say innocent, of the ancient life of the family, and certainly of the ancient life on the farm.

When a townsman first sees these things directly and intimately, he does not despise them as dull but rather dreads them as wild, as he sometimes takes a tame cow for a wild bull. The most obvious example is the hearth which is the heart of the home. A man living in the lukewarm air of centrally-heated hotels may be said to have never seen fire. Compared to him the housewife at the fireside is an Amazon wrestling with a flaming dragon. The same moral might be drawn from the fact that the watchdog fights while the wild dog often runs away. Of the husband, as of the house-dog, it may often be said that he has been tamed into ferocity.

This is especially true of the sort of house represented by the country cottage. It is only in theory that the things are petty and prosaic; a man realistically experiencing them will feel them to be things big and baffling and involving a heavy battle with nature. When we read about cabbages or cauliflowers in the papers, and especially the comic papers, we learn to think of them as commonplace. But if a man of any imagination will merely consent to walk round the kitchen-garden for himself, and really looks at the cabbages and cauliflowers, he will feel at once that they are vast and elemental things like the mountain in the clouds. He will feel something almost monstrous about the size and solidity of the things swelling out of that small and tidy patch of ground. There are moods in which that everyday English kitchen plot will affect him as men are affected by the reeking wealth and toppling rapidity of tropic vegetation; the green bubbles and crawling branches of a nightmare.

But whatever his mood, he will see that things so large and work so laborious cannot possibly be merely trivial. His reason no less than his imagination will tell him that the fight here waged between the family and the field is of all things the most primitive and fundamental. If that is not poetical, nothing is poetical, and certainly not the dingy Bohemianism of the artists in the towns. But the point for the moment is that even by the purely artistic test the same truth is apparent. An artist looking at these things with a free and a fresh vision will at once appreciate what I mean by calling them wild rather than tame. It is true of fire, of water, of vegetation, of half a hundred other things. If a man reads about a pig, he will think of something comic and commonplace, chiefly because the word "pig" sounds comic and commonplace. If he looks at a real pig in a real pigsty, he will have the sense of something too large to be alive, like a hippopotamus at the Zoo.

This is not a coincidence or a sophistry; it rests on the real and living logic of things. The family is itself a wilder thing than the State; if we mean by wildness that it is born of will and choice as elemental and emancipated as the wind. It has its own laws, as the wind has; but properly understood it is infinitely less subservient than things are under the elaborate and mechanical regulations of legalism. Its obligations are love and loyalty, but these are things quite capable of being in revolt against merely human laws; for merely human law has a great tendency to become merely inhuman law. It is concerned with events that are in the moral world what cyclones and earthquakes are in the material world.

People are not born in an infant-school any more than they die in an undertaker's shop. These prodigies are private things; and take place in the tiny theatre of the home. The public systems, the large organisation, are a mere machinery for the transport and distribution of things; they do not touch the intrinsic nature of the things themselves. If a birthday present is sent from one family to another all the legal system, and even all that we call the social system, is only concerned with the present so long as it is a parcel. Nearly all our modern sociology might be called the philosophy of parcels. For that matter nearly all our modern

descriptions of Utopia or the Great State might be called
the paradise of postmen. It is in the inner chamber that the
parcel becomes a present; that it explodes, so to speak,
into its own radiance and real popularity; and it is equally
true, so far as that argument is concerned, whether it is
a bon-bon or a bomb. The essential message is always a
personal message; the important business is always private
business. And this is, of course, especially with the first of
all birthday presents which presents itself at birth; and it is
no exaggeration to talk of a bomb as the symbol of a baby.
Of course, the same is true of the tragic as of the beatific
acts of the domestic drama; of the spadework of the struggle for life or the Damoclean sword of death.

The defence of domesticity is not that it is always happy,
or even that it is always harmless. It is rather that it does
involve, like all heroic things, the possibilities of calamity
and even of crime. Old Mother Hubbard may find that
the cupboard is bare; she may even find a skeleton in the
cupboard. All that is involved here is the insistence on
the true case for this intimate type of association; that in
itself it is certainly not commonplace and most certainly is
not conventional. The conventions belong rather to those
wider worldly organisations which are now set up as rivals
to it; to the club, to the school and above all to the State.
You cannot have a successful club without rules; but a
family will really do without rules exactly in proportion
as it is a successful family. What somebody said about the
songs of a people could be said much more truly about
the jokes of a household. And a joke is in its nature a wild
and spontaneous thing; even the modern fanaticism for
organisation has never really attempted to organise laughter like a chorus. Therefore, we may truly say that these
external emblems or examples of something grotesque
and extravagant about our private possessions are not mere

artistic exercises in the incongruous; they are not, as the phrase goes, mere paradoxes. They are really related to the aboriginal nature of the institution itself and the idea that is behind it. The real family is something as wild and elemental as a cabbage.

POSTLUDE

A Closing Thought from G. K. Chesterton

Either the Catholic civilization must be restored or it must be scrapped. So I do indeed call for a revival, a common sense revival, in defence of justice, freedom, property, and the family.

("The Revival I Want," 1933)